EVEN ME: MAINTAINING FAITH IN UNCERTAIN TIMES

-MARC RABY-

I0145411

> "Please don't miss me, Lord. Please don't forget me, Lord.
> Here I am, Father, and I'm sticking by your side. God, I
> need Your grace, so when You call the others unto You,
> please, God, don't leave my name out." …
>
> *Even Me*
>
> *-Marc Raby*

Even Me: Maintaining Faith In Uncertain Times
Copyright © 2010 Marcus Raby
Published by AMRAE Publishing Group a division of AMRAE Ministries Inc., Birmingham, AL 35202
ISBN: 978-0983391012
Printed and bound in the United States of America
www.amraevision.com

Table Of Contents

Introduction

There is a song, written long ago, that has become quite popular in recent years. It's even been performed in the popular stage play, *Tyler Perry's Madea Goes to Jail.*

The song I'm talking about is entitled, "Lord, I Hear of Showers of Blessing," or, more popularly known as, "Even Me." Now, I'm certain that if you have ever been, or perhaps still are, a member of a hymnal-based worship service, whether Baptist, charismatic, or even non-denominational, you may recall it.

This is one of those songs that declares a humble spirit, hungry for something from God. Let me say that I believe that that's an awesome combination; to be both humble *and* hungry for more of God. As I reflected on the song and its powerful lyrics, it began to consume my heart with a grateful spirit.

Now, I've got to be honest and tell you that there really isn't anything "super deep" or "super spiritual" about this song. However, I do believe it conveys the hearts of many believers in the Body of Christ. It's just a powerful and simple plea.

If I were to paraphrase the song, which was written in the 1860's by Elizabeth Codner & William B. Bradbury (see page 113), it would say something like: "Father, I've been hearing good stuff about what

You have going on in the world. And, Father, I see that You're doing it for lots of people everywhere. I see that You are really making a way for people who can't seem to find a way out of no way. So, Father, can You please do that for me as well? I'm messed up, too. Please don't miss me, Lord. Please don't forget me, Lord. Here I am, Father, and I'm sticking by your side. God, I need Your grace, so when You call the others unto You, please, God, don't leave my name out."

Now, does any of that sound familiar to you? Throughout the song, the writers continue to expand on the love of God, how pure and unchanging that love is. It shows that they, even as they pour their hearts into this melody, have no doubt about how good God is or how powerful He is.

The songwriters have reached a place where they are being very real and transparent with God by expressing, "God, I know how powerful and how easily accessible Your blood is. I know Your grace is sufficient, and I know it's mighty. But, Father, I need You to magnify all of those things in my life. I need You to strengthen me by taking those things and helping me to make them bigger than the bad, the negative, and the grief that's going on around and even inside me."

Now, if any of those pleas resonate with you, then you're the one I believe God is calling me to speak to through this literature. I don't want to be "super spiritual" in what I'm sharing through this book. But, I do hope to highlight those vital necessities for a peaceful life and a courageous walk in faith during what may be a difficult time in your life.

Read on and be blessed.

God Is Gracious...

You know, much like the authors of "Even Me," many of us recognize that God is all-powerful, all-seeing, and all-knowing. Sometimes, though, with all that's going on in the world, it may seem as if God overlooks us in the process of Him doing all His wondrous works. **Not true!**

We may even get to a place where it seems as if we're beyond remedy or help. **Definitely, not true!**

You see, the reason we do this is because we have a small view of Who God is. We have an even smaller view of what He can actually do in our lives. We put our world perspective on God and determine within our hearts that He can't possibly help us. We feel insignificant and think that God can't possibly care about what we are individually going through.

We look at God and determine that He is more concerned with the world-at-large than with Mary, Sam, and Marc. **Completely not true!**

I know I've asked myself at times: *Why would God want to get involved in, or even be bothered with, my many issues?*

Yes, I have issues!

The truth is, according to Romans 3:23, we all have them. In fact, we have so many issues God had to come up with a solution. That's why He sent Himself to rescue us from ourselves.

And, you know the really great thing about that? God is **still** gracious and good enough to step into our messed-up world and give us what we need to endure.

It is of the Lord's mercies that we are not consumed, because His compassions fail not. (Lamentations 3:22)

Gracious – Merciful; Compassionate.

God is gracious. He is merciful and compassionate toward us because He loves us. We are His creation and He cares for us as no other will!

When Jesus, God in the flesh, stepped into our world and lived as we did, He did it for the sole purpose of being able to identify with His creation and to deal with our issues. The only way He could identify was to come down from Heaven in the form of an imperfect creature, yet, without sin. Jesus walked the Earth checking out the actions of mankind so that He could become the solution we all needed.

That solution was for Him to present Himself on the Cross at Calvary. Once He presented Himself for the entire world, He opened the way for man to appear before God. And, He did it in such a way that we would not have to go through any other channels other than Him.

I am the Way, the Truth, and the Life. No man cometh unto the Father but by Me. (John 14:6)

Jesus threw open the doors of the temple so we could have complete and total access to God the Father. There is no veil, no bridge, or door to keep us from having complete fellowship with God at any time for as long as we choose.

There's a guarantee for every child of God, and it is this: **God always assures us an audience of One.** We should never feel as if we are competing with others for God's attention. It may be hard to understand or believe, but God is big enough to go around. He is an awesome God!

If the entire population of the world were to sit on God's lap all at the same time, we would ALL fit! Isn't that wonderful? He is **HUGE!** He can accommodate all of us! How do you think His Spirit inhabits all our prayers and praise at the same time? Each of us can be filled with His precious Holy Spirit all at once!

We truly, always, get His undivided attention. He has promised that He is *always* with us and will *never* leave nor forsake us. These are promises we know He will keep because He keeps His promises to us in all things.

Let us hold fast the profession of our faith without wavering; (for He is faithful that promised) (Hebrews 10:23)

We should also bear in mind that God is His Word. Because of that fact, He can find nothing or no one greater than Him to swear by. When He swears on His Word, He swears on Himself. He gives us His Word, Himself, and we can fully trust in Him. If God was called to be a witness in the Court of Life, He would place His hand on Himself and say, *"So help Me, Me!"*

In the beginning was the Word, and the Word was with God and the Word was God... (John 1:1)

As we believe on Him and His Word, we discover that it is easier to draw closer to Him. Indeed, as we draw closer to God, He draws closer to us. He waits for the time when we will turn around and realize that He is for us and not against us. He waits for the moment when we realize that, no matter what we do, He has been waiting for us to come to our senses. He wants us to turn around and consider Him and all that He is and can be in our lives. He wants to be in our lives in a huge way. He is waiting.

Now, by the same token, if we pull away from Him, our actions will cause a void to come between us and Him. It will seem as though He has turned or walked away from us because we are caught up in the cares of the world and the desires of our hearts. But, He said He will never leave nor forsake us.

When we turn from God, however briefly, it may seem that He is nowhere to be found as we try to include Him in the things that **we** want to do. But, if we put down our ways, our desires, and turn around, we will find that He has never left us. Simple but true.

Consider the examples He has given us in the Bible. We never see God force Himself on anyone. He is kind and gracious. He allows us to make the choice of pushing toward or pulling away from Him.

Look at the parable of the lost or, prodigal, son in Luke Chapter 15. At a certain point in time, this young man requested his inheritance from his father. This was obviously not the best thing for him at that particular time; he wasn't ready. But, the father loved his son enough to allow him to find his way in whatever manner he chose. Believe it or not, God loves us like that.

Well, as the story goes, the young man wasted all of his inheritance. Because he ran out of money, he had to get a job with a farmer. His job was feeding the swine. The young man sank to such an inglorious low, that he wished he could fill his belly with the same slop the hogs ate! That's when he came to his senses.

Just like the father in the parable, God doesn't want us to get our inheritance and pull away from Him. He only wants us to draw closer so that we can have the benefit of **ALL** of His goodness.

When that young man came to his senses, he went back to his father. His father received him with a happy heart and even threw a party for his rebellious son. God wants to do the same for us!

He knows the things we are going to go through as we strive toward maturity. He knows that, in many instances, experience will be our greatest teacher. That is, until we come to the place in which we will allow His Holy Spirit to instruct us. That's why He desires that we make the right decisions in everything we do.

By His choice, God has equipped us with a will. God doesn't want puppets serving Him; puppets only move when moved. They are controlled by the strings supporting them.

God created us to be like Him. He equipped us with brains, minds, hearts and emotions so that we can make decisions and freely serve Him; if we choose. Therefore, utilizing the will He equipped us with, either we draw closer to Him or not. The choice is entirely ours.

Whether we will or will not serve God, the choice is entirely up to us. God's graciousness will not change one way or the other. He constantly pulls us toward Himself with loving-kindness.

God wants to maintain a close relationship with each of us so that we can experience His power in our lives in every given situation. He desires that we place all our burdens upon Him because He cares about all the things we go through.

Unfortunately, just like the prodigal son, when we try to personally control our situation, vexation often comes. We seek this control at times by trying to figure out how, why, even when, God will intervene. Because many of us really can't comprehend God giving us the kind of one-on-one attention He desires to give to us, we have a difficult time understanding the goodness of God in His totality.

The truth is, we will never be able to really and truly wrap our minds around just how great our God is . . . and that's OK. He has already showed us in His Word that His ways are not our ways; neither are His thoughts our thoughts. God's ways are so much higher than ours it is virtually impossible for us to understand *how* He can do the things He does in our lives.

Imagine the doubts and other emotions the Children of Israel experienced as they stood at the edge of the Red Sea. The Egyptians were behind them and nothing but water in front of them. They didn't know what to do. This apparently weak man, Moses, sent to lead them out of captivity didn't appear to be much of a leader. Yet, God...

What's that you have in your hands, Moses?

The rod you gave me, Lord.

Well, what are you waiting for? Lift up the rod and stretch out your hand!! (Exodus 14:15 – 16)

God called Moses and his brother Aaron to perform many miracles for Pharaoh's benefit. These miracles were designed to cause Pharaoh to release the Children of Israel.

The same rod had turned into a serpent and then swallowed up the serpents that the magicians conjured up. But, when Moses came to the water's edge, he obviously forgot just how powerful God had already been.

Amazingly enough, considering how big, awesome, and powerful God is, our limited ability to know who God is can many times keep Him from showing us who He is in our situations. Our limited ability will keep God in a virtual box. That box will prevent Him from working on our situation in the way He desires. If we choose not to trust fully in Him and decide, instead, to depend on our own wisdom and knowledge, we may achieve disastrous results.

Fortunately, for the Children of Israel, Moses had the faith to follow God's command. As soon as he raised the rod, the water pushed back and allowed the Israelites to cross over on dry ground. Guess what? God is asking you the same question and giving you the same command:

Lift up what I have given to you and stretch out your hand!

And He accomplishes it all in His good time for your life. God graciously orchestrates events in your life so that He will receive the greatest glory and it will work out for your greatest good. God does not work on a time clock.

He doesn't punch the clock every day saying, "OK, time to work on Marc's problem for the next eight hours. Phew! I'll be glad when this day is over!"

God always works on point! He takes care of our situation and moves on to the next event. He does this because He loves us and wants the best for us.

NOTE: We are the ones who continually bring up negative situations over and over again, wasting precious time instead of moving with God.

Also, we can't allow ourselves to assume that God owes us anything. When we do this, the very act places us in a position of being ungrateful. It causes us to think **we** can control the things God does in our lives. *We cannot control God!*

I know: sometimes the situations we encounter may seem unfair. Sometimes we may even feel as if we are in our very own "Job" experience. I well understand that frustration!

In fact, it was a little over a year ago that my own mother, Minister Rita F. Raby, passed away as a result of kidney failure.

You know, for quite some time I was very angry with the Lord.

How could He take my mother, my nurturer, my support, my hope—how could He take her from me?

I went into my own spill with the Lord. **And I was angry!**

Here was a woman who had been faithful to the Lord, loyally serving Him and His people all her life. She had given unselfishly of herself to so many people!

I remember thinking, ***How could You take her like this?***

I remember interceding for her with my prayer. I recall singing a song of healing over her in an attempt to elevate my faith to where I felt it needed to be in order for her to live. I even decreed the Word of God for her to be healed.

One day, while sitting with her at the hospital, I remember singing, *"You are the Lord, that healeth me, you are the Lord her healer..."*

And as I began to worship the Lord through this song, my mom began to sing a new song, her own song! As she sang, I came to realize where her faith was.

There is a traditional hymn, beautifully performed by Douglas Miller, entitled, "My Soul's Been Anchored in the Lord." My mother, who had often found great delight in worshipping the Lord with these words, began to sing,

...Though the storms keep on raging in my life,
And sometimes it's hard to tell the night from day,
Still that hope that lies within is reassured.
As I keep my eyes upon the distant shore,
I know He'll lead me safely to that blessed place He has prepared.

But if the storms don't cease,

And if the winds keep on blowing in my life,

My soul has been anchored in the Lord.

I gotta tell you --- I was so confused!

I couldn't understand **why** my mother, despite her suffering and pain, still found such a delight in the Lord! It just didn't seem fair!

Then I realized that my mother had no doubt in her mind of how great God was to her. I recognized that, despite what it looked like to me on the outside, God's plan was marvelous to her on the inside. I watched her faith and her worship.

It began to minister to me in a way like never before! Here was a woman who, in my opinion, didn't have a thing in the world to be grateful for! Yet, she was.

She was thankful just that God was God. She showed me that, no matter what I'm faced with, if there is nothing else to delight in, I can nonetheless delight in the fact that *God is still God.*

Sure, I miss my mother. And yes, it hurts at times to know that she's gone. But, I have to agree with her that God is still great. I could go on and on about what losing such a great woman of God taught me. Instead, I want you to remember, most of all, that, no matter what you're faced with, **God is greater still!** When you get to the point where it seems a situation is just unbearable, just know that He's greater than everything!

Romans 11:33-36 (Amplified Bible) puts it best:

Oh, the depth of the riches and wisdom and knowledge of God! How unfathomable (inscrutable, unsearchable) are His judgments (His decisions)! And how untraceable (mysterious, undiscoverable) are His ways (His methods, His paths)! For who has known the mind of the Lord and who has understood His thoughts, or who has [ever] been His counselor? Or who has first given God anything that he might be paid back or that he could claim recompense? For from Him and through Him and to Him are all things. [For all things originate with Him and come from Him; all things live through Him, and all things center in and tend to consummate and to end in Him.] To Him be glory forever! Amen (so be it).

If we keep this passage of scripture in mind, it will create or reinforce in us a positive mindset telling us that what we are going through is only part of a greater picture. It is a picture designed to show a better view of who God is in and through us.

Even knowing that God owes us nothing, He has still extended a great promise for our lives.

For I know the thoughts that I think toward you, said the LORD, thoughts of peace, and not of evil, to give you an expected end. (Jeremiah 29:11AKJV)

There are no limits to what God can and will do. He is literally "off the chain!"

If you believe that, and operate as though you believe that, then you'll see Him move how He chooses to move in your life. You'll see Him fulfill His promises for your life.

I will caution you to know that it may not be *quite* how you planned for Him to move. You might hope for Him to change your situation, when really all that may be needed is for Him to change you in the situation. Remember Jeremiah 29:11 --- He knows what He's doing!

...Also Faithful

...because His compassions fail not. They are new every morning: great is Thy faithfulness. (Lamentations 3:22b – 23)

Because God is gracious, we also find that He is faithful. These are only two of the traits in His character we are encouraged to draw from.

Since He is faithful, we can know that He has no problem doing His part in our lives. Always at work in our lives, God does what needs to be done so we can fulfill the destiny He has called us to.

Think about it: every morning, before we even think about getting out of bed, God has a new portion of compassion prepared just for us. It doesn't matter how badly we messed up yesterday. It doesn't matter how badly we will mess up today. When we ask Him to forgive us for the mess ups in our lives, He does. He continually shows compassion to us because of how much He loves us. Because He is God, His faithfulness is always with us. His faithfulness is enough for every need we can ever have in our lives.

Now, although He does His part and works for our good, we still have to build up our own faith. Our faith does not have to match God's faithfulness; it never will. Our faith has to grow. We have to activate our faith in a way that will let Him know we are exercising the faith muscles He has equipped us with.

Faith muscles? What's that?

This concept may sound and seem strange to you, but, bear with me. God has equipped each of us with faith muscles.

Consider the muscles in your body. Lack of use can cause your muscles to become useless. If you don't take care of your muscles, they become weak and will not work. They will not function in the way they are supposed to function.

When you need them, they may not be able to do the things you need them to do. Diseases such as MS can also cause the muscles in your body to malfunction. Diseases of this type can make a person's muscles as well as his or her limbs useless in many cases.

Our body's muscles are designed to fulfill certain tasks. Our arm and shoulder muscles help us lift and carry; these muscles are not designed to help us lift and carry the cares of the world! Our leg and hip muscles aid us in walking and running; but, not away from God! (I just wanted to add that in there.) Our abdominal muscles assist us in bending, walking and helps to support our back and trunk.

Our faith muscles serve similar purposes. By God's design, our faith muscles are not designed just to help us overcome obstacles. These muscles are also designed to help us lift the shield of faith, bear under the spiritual weight of the breastplate of righteousness, and effectively use the Sword of the Spirit which is the Word of God.

Look at what Apostle John tells us:

Ye are of God, little children, and have overcome them: because greater is He that is in you, than He that is in the world. (I John 4:4)

We have to have faith to believe that God operates in and through us as we live our lives. Our faith muscles are available to us because the greater One, God through Jesus Christ, lives inside of us.

Now, if we don't develop our faith muscles, we will not be able to overcome the many trials and tribulations we go through. Our tiny strength is not equipped for it. Fortunately, with the greater One inside of us, we become more than conquerors **through** Him that loves us.

Look at it this way: You are a cross-country runner on the Track of Life. You have been running for a long time; seems like all your Christian life! When you started out, you felt great.

Your muscles were primed, your mind set, and your heart fastened on the end of your journey. At first, you enjoyed the changing scenery as you ran. Green, lush grass with maybe a slight breeze to cool you as you ran along. Oh, look! There's a small stream running alongside your path! How peaceful!

While running your race, you begin to notice other participants. Perhaps many of them ran along with you in the beginning. Then, some of them dropped out of the race – they couldn't handle the race or the pressure. Then, there were those who ran in front of you and left you in their dust (not good to your way of thinking!)

All of a sudden, the path takes an upward turn. That's all right; you trained for this change. Although your breathing becomes a bit labored, you know what to do. You know how to pump the muscles in your arms and legs to get that needed little burst so you can continue without slowing down. Your path plateaus and you are able to catch your breath, your second wind.

Look at you! You're headed downhill now! Wow! You pick up a little speed here and make up for the small amount of time lost while going up the hill. Many others seem to have dropped out; they quit. More and more are dropping like flies.

You feel good! You trained for this race! You know how to keep going! And you do.

But, what's this? The terrain changes again; drastically this time. Where there had been a smooth path, there are now potholes, rocks, gravel and loose sand among other obstacles on your path. It's all uphill now! And, it's wearing you down! The party is over!

You try to focus; you attempt to remain true to your training. Then, the unimaginable happens: you stumble and fall! You lose your footing as well as your focus! You forget your training! Your confidence hesitates: in yourself and in God.

You forget that God has called you to this particular cross-country event. You forget how hard you trained!

"It's so unfair! Why did the terrain change so drastically? God, I thought You *wanted* me to win! Why? Why?! **WHY!?!?!?!**"

Has God's plan for your life changed? Has your assignment been recalled? No to all the above. There are some things you need to consider at this point.

1.   The assignment is still the same.

2.   The path is still the same.

3.   God is still the same.

*It **is** of the Lord's mercies that we are **not consumed**, because **His compassions fail not**. They are **new EVERY morning: great is Thy faithfulness**. (Lamentations 3:22 – 23)*

You see, while you are running the Cross-Country of Life, God has an over-head view of the entire race. He sees every twist and turn ahead of you. He knows every bump and scrape you will receive. He watches to see **how** you will react.

When my mother passed away, I had much the same discussion with God, the main question: WHY?

"Why, God? Why would you take **my** Mama? (Yes, I took it personally!) Look at how faithful she's been to you? Look at all she has done for Your Kingdom, Lord! God, You could have healed her!"

My rant came from the very depths of my soul! It hurt so badly! He took my best friend, my mentor, my first girlfriend! I blamed Him because I didn't understand. I was on the Cross-Country Track of Life and I stumbled and fell! I hit the biggest pothole of my life! *And God allowed it!*

Not because He was angry with me or my mother. He didn't even do it just because He could! God used this tragedy in my life to cause me to grow more in Him. He wanted me to become more faithful to Him. He wanted me to have more faith in Him.

I know; that's hard. Doesn't make much sense, does it? Many of the things we go through in life are designed to cause us to come into a deeper place with God; a place of more understanding. In the same way we want **ALL** the blessings he can give to us, God wants **ALL** of us that we can give to Him.

What if I had become so angry with God that I couldn't find my way back to the Cross-Country Track of Life? What if I had just thrown my hands in the air and given up?

God's purposes for my life would have probably gone unfulfilled. He gives us choices: either we will fulfill or we won't. He loves us enough to allow us to accept or reject the assignments He has for our lives. Had I given up, He would have had to either find someone else to do what He called me to do or…

Sometimes the thing God has called us to do is just for us; there is no substitute. There are lives we have to touch personally. There are blessings we personally have to give to other people. He has created us for such a time as this to fulfill **His** purposes.

Just a quick aside: Remember Queen Esther? She was called for such a time in her life. At just the right time to do the most good, God placed Esther in a high position to save her people from death and destruction.

It was not convenient. It was not something she was prepared to do. It might not have been something she even **wanted** to do! She was quite comfortable going to the King only when he called; nothing more, nothing less.

But, that was not the purpose God had for Esther! He called her to be a type of Savior to her people. The same call is upon your life in much the same way! Can I just say right here: God has not called us to be ordinary but extra-ordinary!

That's why God remains faithful when we are faithless. He will not change His integrity no matter what happens in our lives.

Now, in no way can we match the faithfulness of God. But, we can take up the cause of God in our own way. We may not understand the *Why* of what God does in our lives. We may not even understand His timing. That's OK. God has a plan and we are all a part of that plan.

As He is faithful, He wants us to be faithful and follow Him. Stumbling and falling hurts. They are very embarrassing distractions in our lives. However, they are also part of God's plan for our lives.

Your question, at this point, may be, "How do I recover from the catastrophe of stumbling and falling?" Well, here's part of the solution.

1. **Remember: the greater One is 'in' you.** He has never left you; He never will. He sees you running, He sees the twists and turns that throw you off, He sees when you stumble and fall. But…

    > *The steps of a good man are ordered by the Lord: and He delighteth in his way. Though he fall, he shall not be utterly cast down: for the Lord upholdeth him with His hand. (Psalms 37:23 – 24)*

    Pastor Donnie McClurkin said very simply, "We fall down but we get up!" When you stumble and fall, God's desire is not for you to stay in that place: there is no victory in staying down! He wants you to get up!

    You can count on God to lift you up and dust you off. Then, he will push you back on to the track. He won't allow you to quit! He's in it to win it! *Are you?*

2. **Don't just pick up the Shield of Faith! Get it all!** You wouldn't wear just one sock or shoe, would you? Would you

play baseball without a glove? Would you try to hit the baseball with a broom handle? Probably not! Then, it doesn't make much sense for us to try to use only certain pieces of the whole Armor of God when we go into battle.

The full Armor of God has to be used in whole, not in part! You are in a spiritual battle. When you step out of your house in the morning, an unseen force waits for you. This force will try you, trip you up, and attempt to make you fall. It is to be expected since the main job of the enemy of our souls is to steal our joy, to kill our desire to win, and to destroy our faith.

The full Armor of God will allow you to engage the enemy in a full frontal battle on a continuing basis. And, don't forget your faith muscles!

As you put on the helmet of salvation, your faith muscles enable you to wear the breastplate of righteousness, hold up the shield of faith and slice with the Sword of the Spirit, the Word of God. And when you need to endure in prayer, your faith muscles support your spirit.

As you read *Ephesians 6:10 – 18*, you will find that God desires that we put all of His Armor on; we are not to pick and choose. We need it all!

Become an expert with your equipment! When you use the full Armor of God on a daily basis, you become better in your warfare. And it shows! The enemy will be afraid of you! He will hate when you wake up in the morning!

3. **Read the Word of God daily.** Renew your mind! Think of your Bible as your textbook for life. As you read and absorb the Word of God, you are able to see how to pass each and every test or tribulation you encounter! Now, I didn't say the tests or tribulations would be easy. However, the Word will give you what you need to make it through to the next season in your life.

   We need the Word of God to guide us through all of life's difficulties. The Word of God is our roadmap as we travel the paths of life. As we read the Word, God is able to give us insight and direction so we can make it to the next intersection in our lives.

   Thy Word is a lamp unto my feet and a light unto my path. (Psalms 119:105)

We have to develop a love for the Word of God. In the end, it is only His Word that will bring us into a good place, a land flowing with milk and honey.

I'm not quite finished with the Cross-Country Race analogy. Let's talk about some of the obstacles you will encounter during your Race. Many of these obstacles will cause you to stumble and fall in your faith.

Living in the D Zone!

King Solomon wrote that there is no new thing under the sun. As we look at our world today, we see the truth behind his statement.

During the 1920s and 1930s, our world faced a period of devastating recession. Wealthy people, losing vast quantities of riches, committed suicide. They couldn't stand against the pressure of coming poverty.

Already in the 2000s, we again face a period of devastating recession. Billionaires, finding it hard to maintain their way of living when their financial worth drops down into the millions, commit suicide. Job and income loss cause men and women to murder their families and commit suicide. Why? So they will not become a burden on society!

Famine, poverty, lack in some form, at some point in the lifetime of the world as we see it, has previously occurred.

Follow along with me as I continue on the Cross-Country Track of Life.

The track I speak of is circular. A circle surrounds each of us every day of our lives. As we go through life, the diameter of our particular track tends to change and grow with us. Interesting, isn't it?

Look at it this way: when you were born, you began running on the Track of Life. You go through all the different seasons of development for the rest of your life. As you grow, you pass through different zones. These zones are designed to give you what you need for that particular season so you can move forward and grow more.

Your "A" zone may include such things as Academics, Adulthood, Arthritis, and Arrests. Similarly, the "B" zone may include such events as Babies, Booze, Spiritual Blindness, etc. The "C" zone may include College, Cancer, and Career. But, I want to show you what often takes place in the "D" zone of our lives.

As you run on the Cross-Country Track of Life, you are destined to encounter obstacles: ditches, potholes, cliffs, mountains, jungles, and other areas designed to hinder your progress. Now, though, let's give some of these hindrances names.

First of all, let's be clear of what a hindrance is. By definition, hindrance, according to the 2005 Merriam-Webster Thesaurus, is, *something that makes movement or progress more difficult; something that stands in the way of one's progress or achievement.*

Of course, this could also mean someone; a person. This person could be friend or foe. It might be a parent, a sibling or other relative, a friend, or an associate. God can use people to push you forward. He can also use the same person to cause you to push forward as you discover how to negotiate in the destiny He has carved out for you.

Now, nothing in the definition says that the hindrance, person or thing, **cannot** be moved out of the way. A hindrance could very well be a **temporary setback** which will cause the person who is hindered to *recalculate* or *recalibrate* the direction in which he or she is headed. Hindrances can be used for your good. Or, if you wallow in the pity pool long enough, it can lead to your not-so-good.

And we know that all things work together for good to them that love God, to them who are the called according to His purpose. (Romans 8:28)

Understand this, not all hindrances are meant for death. God will allow hindrances so you can grow. He allows some hindering opportunities to cause you to stretch and move in ways you otherwise would not have moved. Many hindrances will cause you to come up with a different plan so you can move around the obstacle in a different way.

As Romans 8:28 signifies, ALL things are working together for our good because we love God and we are called according to HIS purpose. This means that God will throw us into different situations so we will get to our destination in His glory.

We have to have faith that this is true. We can't doubt any part of His Word. It is all true; it is all relevant. Everything God has for you will come forward when God **SAYS** for it to come forward.

Needless to say, you are not on the Track of Life by yourself. As we saw in the previous section, there are those who will fall behind you on the track, those who will run beside you and still those who will run ahead of you. Unfortunately, there are also those who will try to push you off the track.

Many of the hindrances you face in the D Zone while running on the Track of Life will come to you from three different sources:

1. You

2. Others

3. The Enemy of our souls

Wherefore seeing we also are compassed about with so great a cloud of witnesses, let us lay aside every weight, and the sin which doth so easily beset us, and let us run with patience the race that is set before us... (Hebrews 12:1)

Everyone is watching you. Not just the folks you see in the natural. But, also those persons you can't see. The Bible is filled with witnesses who are, more than likely, watching from Heaven to see how we perform on the Track of Life. They are rooting for us!

Our greatest cheerleaders, The Father, The Son, and The Holy Spirit, always cheer us on as we come to each zone, each season. They want us to cross the finish line triumphantly! God, in these three personalities, repeatedly feeds instruction to us as we run. He reveals new strategies to us, increasing our chances of success. He will not allow us to run this race alone!

When we encounter obstacles on the Track of Life, the Word of God instructs us how to defeat or move those obstacles out of our way. Let's look at some of the common obstacles.

Discouragement

One of the first obstacles you may run into on the Cross-Country Track of Life is discouragement.

"You'll never win. Our family has never won that race."

"You can't win because someone else will beat you."

There are many people with you on the Track of Life who *supposedly* encourage you. Instead, these well-meaning folks send out words of *encouragement* with an underlying tone of *discouragement* causing you to *doubt* yourself. When you start *doubting* yourself, you eventually *doubt* God who placed you on the track in the first place.

Run away quickly from these folks! You must avoid them at all costs so that they will not hinder your progress!

Even if you find yourself in a ditch on the side of the Track, you have to pull yourself out of the ditch. Get your mind back on the race so you can continue to move forward! God will help you. He is always there with you every step of the way. He encourages you because He knows you have everything you need to move forward in Him.

Distraction

"We need money to pay our bills. You can't go to work for the Lord! He doesn't pay that much!"

"If you don't graduate from college in this particular field that your Great-Granddaddy Clyde graduated in, you will never make it!"

These are *distractions*. It is important to stay focused. Everything has a perfect time and season. Even God has a good, an acceptable, and a perfect will for your life.

You know what you are supposed to do in your lifetime on the earth; you have known for as long as you can remember. But, other folks are checking you out. They see what *they* think is the best path for you to follow. These well-meaning folks give you a destiny and a destination because it's what *they* want in your life. (They desire to live their lives *through* you!)

They feel that what they "*see*" is what you are supposed to do. These folks and the situations they create in your life will distract you from moving forward. If allowed, they will permanently hinder you from accomplishing the goals God has set for you to accomplish. You may find yourself at the age of 80 unfulfilled because you did not pursue what God had for you; you pursued what others thought you should pursue!

Diversion

"Well, you should do this for a while and then you can go back to that... if you want to."

"Let's get married while we are in college. We'll be careful so we won't have any babies..."

"You need to step off your path, just for a minute, and then you can go back and accomplish so much more!"

While you are running on the Track of Life, some people will intentionally place *logs* across the track. These obstructions will cause you to have to go around and not straight through. These logs may show up in the form of dead-end jobs, business opportunities, or ministries not designed for you according to what God has in mind for you.

Hope deferred maketh the heart sick, but when the desire cometh, it is a tree of life. (Proverbs 13:12)

When you don't follow the track in the way God desires, you become ill-at-ease and confused. You lose your focus and become misdirected. Your heart is sick because you realize you aren't doing what God has called you to do. Unless the log is too big for you to jump over, you must get back on track as quickly as possible so you can get to your desire.

Division

Joseph had a dream. His dream, from God, told him that one day he would be ruler over his entire family. His brothers hated him because of that dream! They wanted to kill him; anything to stop that dream from taking place.

You have a dream: you desire to complete the Cross-Country Track of Life so that your Ruler can say to you, *"Well done, thou good and faithful servant... Enter thou into the joy of thy Lord!" (Matthew 25:21)*

Remember that Cloud of Witnesses? Well, the ones you can see are the "Joseph's Brothers" in your life. Many of them can't stand you! They will dig pits into the track you are on so that you can fall into it. They don't want you to succeed! And there is one that hates you more than the ones you see: the **devil!**

These witnesses will sell you into slavery and bondage because they don't want you to accomplish what God has determined for you to accomplish. They will go to great lengths to kill your dream if you let them!

But God will never allow these obstacles to keep you from moving forward. He will not allow these obstructions to keep you from the destiny He has created for you! He has a **D Zone**, as well!

God's D Zone

Dance

When King David finally went into Jerusalem as the King of God's people, he rejoiced. When he was able to bring the Ark of the Covenant into the city, he danced right out of his clothes!

Of course, there were those who despised his actions (his wife who became barren. She dishonored her husband and God by her actions.) David didn't care! He recognized the power and importance of God! He recognized how God had brought him from the sheep yard, through the caves, to the palace as God's chosen King over His people.

On the Cross-Country Track of Life, there will be times in which you will have to dance because that's all you can do. You will have to dance through a stretch of the track that might give you a rough time. The sands of life may cause you to struggle; the rocks and pebbles may get into your shoes causing blisters and calluses. But, if you **dance** as David danced, God will move you forward toward your destiny.

Declare

Declare the Word of God over your life. When well-meaning family, friends, and associates speak death over your race, instead, you speak life. Declare what God says!

I shall not die but live and declare the works of the Lord! (Psalms 118:17)

I can do ALL things through Christ Who gives me strength! (Philippians 4:13)

Many are the afflictions of the righteous (of which I am,) but the Lord is able to deliver me out of them all! (Psalms 34:19)

I am more than a conqueror through Jesus Christ because He loves me! (Romans 8:37)

For I reckon that the sufferings of this present time are not worthy to be compared with the glory which shall be revealed in me. (Romans 8:18)

Even Me!

The promises listed at the end of this book will provide you with more ammunition as you go forward on the Track of Life.

Decree

How do *you* want your race to end? Do you want to just barely make it? Would you like to classified as an *also ran?* Or, do you want to finish in a blaze of God's glory? It's up to you; **entirely!**

Thou shalt also decree a thing, and it shall be established unto thee: and the light shall shine upon thy ways. (Job 22:28)

How you finish or place is determined by what you say and do. You can finish strong by choosing and using the correct words as you run the race. If you decree complete triumph, you will have complete triumph. If you decree that you just want to finish, you are not giving yourself a very good place throughout the race.

Dedicate

Needless to say, you are going to have to dedicate yourself to this race. You can't be in the race one day and out the next. You can't go on vacation just because the road is hard and times are tough. You have to dedicate your life to finishing strong, no matter what!

I am sure you are acquainted with some people who could be so much more than what they currently are. These are the *also ran's*. They had just as much potential as the winners and high placers but petered out because they chose the negative **D Zone** instead of **God's D Zone**.

Believe it or not, these folks can get back into the race and run it well. All they need is encouragement and direction. And so can you! Don't let a temporary setback throw you off your race! God is faithful and able to make you better than ever as you strive to go to the front of the pack! Remember: God knows your strengths and weaknesses. He is able to turn all things around for His glory and your good!

Who knows? Someone else may be observing your performance and what you choose to do may be what gets them back on track!

Delight

Where do you obtain the most pleasure in your life? Your family or friends? Your job? Maybe from school?

Delight thyself also in the Lord; and He shall give thee the desires of thine heart! (Psalms 37:4)

God is waiting for you to find joy and pleasure in the Cross-Country Track of Life He has placed you on. I know; it's hard to do. When you consider the obstacles, the other people, and the enemy, there seems to be more things to get in your way than that are praiseworthy.

He knows there are going to be times in which you will be so *unmotivated* and *depressed* because of the things you will have to endure on the Track. But, He also knows that if you focus your attention on Him and the end result He has for you, you will take great pleasure and receive great joy in just running on the track placed before you.

Everything natural has a spiritual counterpart. Everything negative has a positive counterpart. As you compete on the Cross-Country Track of Life, you determine whether you want to run from a negative or a positive aspect. Running in the negative takes far more energy than running in the positive.

The positive leaves you vitally charged. Being vitally charged enables you to overcome all things and continually move forward. When you are positively charged, the hindrances and obstacles appear small because they are small. They have no power over you. You are able to jump over the obstacles and not miss a beat as you progress from one level to the next!

The negative causes you to be distracted. Negativity takes your focus and drains your energy. If you are drained, you will not do well in the race. You find yourself falling behind. The images of the obstacles become large and consume you. It seems as though you will never make it to the finish line!

Now, let's go into another zone that will cause you to rethink your strategy as you run on the Track of Life. *Stay with me!*

Faith and Fear

If any of you lack wisdom, let him ask of God, that giveth to all men liberally, and upbraideth not; and it shall be given him. But let him ask in faith, nothing wavering. For he that wavereth is like a wave of the sea driven with the wind and tossed. For let not that man think that he shall receive any thing of the Lord. A double minded man is unstable in all his ways. (James 1:5 – 8)

When you were a child, how did you ask for things? Remember asking for that popular doll or action figure? Do you recall how you approached your parent(s) when you wanted that bicycle that every other kid in the neighborhood had? How did you phrase the question?

"Mommy, can I have Malibu Barbie for my birthday? Please?"

"Daddy, can I have a new bicycle? Huh? Can I? Huh?"

" Grandma, Mama won't get me that new cell phone … Whine!"

Once you asked the question and knew in your heart of hearts that the person you asked would move Heaven and Earth to get you what you requested, you left it alone, didn't you? Unless the person said something like, "We'll see," you went on the assumption that what you requested would be given to you, didn't you?

It's because you didn't have a double mind about the matter. You knew you could trust the word of your parent, grandparent,

Godparent, or whoever to provide your need. ...Just as simple as that. You didn't go back again and again to repeat the request. You stood on the belief that what you asked would be given to you. You believed and had faith in the giver.

Why don't we do the same with God? Hmmmmmm? It seems as though that, just because we can't **see** God, we feel He won't be as responsive to our requests as someone we can see.

We assume that because we don't hear Him **say** anything right away He must not understand our need. Maybe we should whine, throw ourselves on the floor, pout and then, only then, will He answer positively.

We have all been there. But, as we see from James 1:5 − 8, if we don't ask in faith, knowing God will answer, we will not receive anything. In fact, if we ask in any way other than the faith way, we will be classified as having a double mind. **Not good!**

Physically, human beings are equipped with a brain that has two sides or lobes. Each lobe, the left and the right, controls different functions.

Now, the brain itself works as a whole controlling our body completely. When the brain ceases to function, the body does also. The brain and the mind are entirely different. The brain can be seen as your subconscious mind because it functions involuntarily. We don't have to tell the brain to make our heart beat or our blood flow through our veins. As long as the brain functions properly, our heart and vital organs operate involuntarily.

But, there is a part of our heart we need to understand a bit better as we run on the Cross Country Track of Life. You see, our brain sees and reacts to whatever we put in front of it.

If our brain sees something that we perceive as being scary or exciting, we feel it in our body. Our heart trembles in reaction to that scary or exciting thing. We feel the hair on our arm or the back of our neck raise as we feel the adrenaline run quickly through our body.

Now, the thing our eyes see and that tells our brain is scary may or may not be, in fact, scary. But, our brain only reacts to the emotion we feed it. We would have to tell our brain that this particular thing is not scary and continually feed this thought to our brain in order for our body to react differently.

Our heart, though, the other, darker side of our heart, will take that thought and run with it. Our heart, the seat of our emotions, can be seen as our conscious mind. Our heart will cause us to react in a way other than the way we should.

Look at it this way: Your best friend in the world makes a silly remark about your job, family, whatever. Now, you and this friend have always made crazy remarks to each other about the same things for as long as you can remember. None of these comments have ever affected either of you. This time is different.

This time, your heart tells you, "He said you aren't going to get promoted on your job because you are not the best at what you do. He said you are going to be replaced because Andrew is much better at what he does than you are."

This is what you have received in your heart even though this is not what your best friend said. And so, you react differently than you ever did before. Your brain has told your body to react coldly to what your friend said. Your mind turns itself off. You lose feeling for your friend because now you perceive that your friend is against you.

Your friend wonders why he hasn't heard from you and decides to call you after a few days. When he calls, you act very coldly toward him because your heart has deceived you brain into thinking that your friend, your best friend, said something he never said!

When the Bible speaks about a person being double minded, we can then understand It is speaking about the subconscious and the conscious mind. The subconscious mind, the brain, tells your arms and legs to move, your veins to pump blood and your heart to beat.

The conscious mind, though, tells you things that can cause setbacks in your life especially if it is not lined up with the subconscious mind.

"You are going to fail."

"You will never have enough."

"Those people are laughing at you."

"God isn't going to come through!"

Since the Bible speaks about the capacity of man to have two minds on any given situation, we may want to give this subject some thought. It proves to be an interesting concept. One would think that our mind, encapsulated in our single body, would always be on the same frequency. Unfortunately, that's not the case. Our mind can either work with us or against us. Let's take the above scripture for example.

Now, according to His Word, if we ask God for wisdom, He will supply our need. He won't say things like, *"You should have had that already!"* or, *"You should have asked sooner!"*

No, God will lavishly give us the wisdom we ask for; abundantly. But...

We have to take the "buts" in the Word of God seriously. When we encounter a "but" statement, whatever comes after that point could make or break us, if you will.

Here, the reader is cautioned to *ask in faith, nothing wavering.* God does not like wishy-washy. God is very particular about how we approach Him. After all, He is God! He desires that we approach Him boldly, yet humbly; faithful not fearful. That brings us to the purpose of this section – ***faith and fear.***

You will run into many hazards and obstacles on the Cross-Country Track of Life. The main, and most treacherous, obstacle you consistently encounter will be... **YOU**. One part of you will acknowledge your ability to win; the other part will say you can't for whatever reason.

You need wisdom to navigate and negotiate this deceitful Obstacle of Life. You have to boldly come before the Throne of Grace to obtain help in your time of need. You also have to boldly confront your double mind so that you can be on the same sheet of music with God and with yourself.

The heart is deceitful above all things, and desperately wicked: who can know it? (Jeremiah 17:9)

There is nothing new about this. David knew it when he told the Lord, *Search me, O God, and know my heart: try me, and know my thoughts: (Psalms 138:23)*

He realized the capacity of his heart to take him into unproven territory. He knew that his heart had the ability to lead him into areas God did not want him to be in. That's what the flesh, the conscious mind, will do.

Paul learned this principal as well.

For they that are after the flesh do mind the things of the flesh; but they that are after the Spirit the things of the Spirit. For to be carnally minded is death; but to be spiritually minded is life and peace. Because the carnal mind is enmity against God: for it is not subject to the law of God, neither indeed can be. So then they that are in the flesh cannot please God. (Romans 8:5 – 8)

We have to line ourselves up with the Word of God so we can be single-minded in our approach to God and how we ask Him for what we need. We must approach God in faith for what we need. Our carnal mind, or flesh, will cause us to approach God in one way whereas our spiritual mind will want to approach God in a totally different manner. We have to line up our spirit and our flesh so that we can be pleasing to God and approach Him in the way He wants us to approach Him.

We can't approach God with a double mind as we run on the Track of Life; it won't work. We have to use total faith. If not, we will not receive anything.

When we flip-flop between fear and faith, God has a hard time supplying what we really need. Instead of confidently pushing forward on the Track, we get stuck. We find ourselves caught between "sure He will" and "maybe He won't."

Why? We lose our confidence. That's what happens when we ask God for something with fear in our hearts. God knows in which way we are asking.

Now, the same way we ask the Lord for wisdom and help to run on the Track of Life is the same way we run on the Track of Life. Think about Peter.

Peter was always in Jesus' face! Every time Jesus started to do something, Peter was right there on the spot. There are very few times in which Peter wasn't involved in something Jesus was involved in. Even to the cross…

One night, after feeding the multitude of 5,000 who had come to hear Him preach, Jesus told the disciples to get into their ship and cross over to Capernaum. The disciples obeyed Him leaving Him to go up into the mountain to pray. As the disciples attempted to cross the Sea of Galilee, however, a storm came up.

The crew had a hard time rowing; they struggled. As they attempted to keep focused on their task, they saw Someone strolling on the water toward them. Now, just as you or I would, they thought it was a spirit. And, it was! Father, Son, and Holy Spirit all wrapped up in One package!

And here is our faithful Peter.

"Who's that?"

"Be of good cheer, Peter. It is I. Be not afraid!"

"Lord, if it is You, then call me out there with You on the water."

"Well, come on!" (Matthew 14:22 – 33)

And Peter did! He stepped out of the ship and into his destiny! My God!

Of course, you know the remaining disciples were fearful and didn't know exactly what to do. Jesus and Peter, one of them, were actually walking on the water! But, Peter had to ask in faith, nothing wavering. He had to believe in his heart of hearts that what he asked Jesus would come to pass in his life. Once he believed in his heart and lined it up with his brain, he found he had no problem walking out of the boat and onto the water! How about you?

As we run on the Cross Country Track of Life God prepares for us, we find ourselves on different legs throughout the event. We could look at it as a Decathlon with many different events

During this season on your Track, you may be called to be on a ship that takes you from place to place. Your ship is on the Sea of Adversity. The Waters of Change come up against you and make it difficult for you to cross over to the other side.

We face many storms on the Cross-Country Track of Life. Throughout the storms, one of the most constructive things we can do to keep our sanity and focus is keep our eye on Jesus as He calmly walks on the Sea of Life without any fear. He is unaffected by the turbulence we experience. He wants us to be undisturbed as well! He wants us to have a single mind!

Jesus has a single mind. His one thought is to bring each of us into a place that we can trust Him without doubt. He is determined to bring us to a place in our lives that we ask Him for something and have the faith to stand and believe that what we have asked for will be done.

Just like Peter when he first stepped out of the ship, we all have to have the mind of Christ. Jesus faced the same dangers Peter perceived he faced; drowning and death. After all, Jesus was a man who could die just as Peter could. But, He also knew what God had purposed Him for. It wasn't His time to die; nor was it Peter's.

The mind of Christ has no fear. It only has thoughts of victory and deliverance. The mind of Christ allows us to be more in line with what God has purposed for our lives. It allows us to not only walk on the water, but also believe He will sustain us while we are out there and take us to the other side. The mind of Christ leaves no room for doubt.

Jesus wants you to step out of the ship and walk on the water with Him! The Sea of Adversity is nothing more than another leg on the Track of Life; we can walk on it and not sink. **We can do it!**

But, we have to ask in faith when we ask Him to call us out there to walk with Him. We need to see something else as well in this whole scenario.

When Peter stepped out of the boat, he had his eyes on Jesus; **only** on Jesus. He looked neither left nor right. He looked straight at Jesus. And while his eyes were on Jesus, *he walked on the water!*

As long as you keep your eyes on Jesus, you can do anything. Nothing shall be impossible for you. You can climb the highest mountains, you can wade the deepest seas; you can do absolutely anything! ...*If you keep your eyes on Him.*

Unfortunately, though, once Peter noticed the waves and listened to the wind blowing around him, he lost his focus, his concentration. He began to sink.

Have you ever noticed - *this is for runners* - as long as you run with your eye on the horizon, you have no problems? /What happens when you look at the ground right in front of you or at your feet? You stumble. The same concept is used in Matthew 14.

As long as Peter kept his eyes on Jesus, he was fine! You can probably imagine Peter gingerly getting out of the boat and standing for a second as the whole concept of him standing on the water gained strength in his mind. As he became more comfortable with the idea, he probably took a step forward toward the Master. As he became more sure-footed, he probably swaggered for a couple of steps before...

"Lord, save me!" (Matthew 14:30)

What happened? Jesus hadn't left him. Jesus hadn't changed His position. He was still the same as when Peter stepped out of the ship. What happened to cause Peter to reach out to Jesus in panic?

He lost his focus. On the Cross-Country Track of Life, we will encounter many things that cause us to lose our focus. The main thing is fear. Fear is a symptom of a much bigger ailment – *Doubt.* Fear has a bad habit of attacking the heart and deceiving it into thinking that something is going on that, in reality, is not.

Peter's heart perceived that the wind and raging water would destroy him. Although Peter knew Jesus was still there and would not let him die, he still feared the unknown.

We fear the unknown. Whenever we go into foreign territory or outside of our comfort zone, fear of the unknown creeps in and causes us to think thoughts contrary to what God has told us. What was Peter's heart told?

The wind is going to overtake you!

You are going to sink!

Jesus can't save you this time because He is too far away!

We have all experienced these lies. These lies are designed to keep us from going forward in what God has for us. These lies are designed to cause us to forget the word that has been stored in our hearts so that we can move forward with the Plan.

But, what has the Word told us?

When thou passest through the waters, I will be with thee; and through the rivers, they shall not overflow thee: when thou walkest through the fires, thou shalt not be burned; neither shall the flame kindle upon thee. (Isaiah 43:2)

There is a reason to shout in Isaiah 43:2!

God promises that, no matter what situation we find ourselves in, He is there with us and will protect us. We will not drown, we will not be overcome, and the fires will not burn us! Hallelujah!

When we allow fear to manifest in our hearts and grow in our lives, we eventually begin to doubt the things in our lives that God has placed there to cause us to mature.

Jesus did not want Peter to fear the wind blowing around him; He wanted Peter to acknowledge His power over the wind. Peter and the other disciples had already witnessed numerous miracles performed by their beloved Teacher. Peter knew Who Jesus was and what He was capable of doing!

Jesus did not want Peter to be afraid of the waves threatening to overcome him as he walked toward Jesus. He wanted Peter to acknowledge the Greater One inside of him. He wanted Peter to realize that he could do anything but fail because of that fact!

And, guess what? God, through Jesus Christ, wants the exact same thing for you! He doesn't want you to fear the wind and the waves you encounter on the Track of Life! He wants you to be able to ask

Him in faith, nothing wavering, for the strength, courage, and confidence to go further and faster than you have ever gone before. He desires to bring you to the destiny He created for your life before the foundations of the world were laid out.

So, if you are in the **F Zone** of life, make it **God's Faith Zone**. You are sure to accomplish great things and move forward to the destiny God has for you.

Word Power

Your words have power... ...The power to build or destroy. ...The power to encourage or discourage. ...The power to open opportunities or close the door of hope. ...The power to bring life or death.

Death and life are in the power of the tongue: and they that love it shall eat the fruit thereof... (Proverbs 18:21)

What do you talk about all day long? What are the first words out of your mouth when you get out of bed in the morning? Are they words that bring life? Hope? Joy? Peace?

Or, are they words that bring destruction? ...Death? ...Anger? ...Turmoil? What words are you speaking over your life?

Someone somewhere right now, this very moment, is saying something about you. They may be words that bring confusion in your life. Or, they just might be words aimed at turning someone against you. They could quite possibly be words that will cause you to doubt yourself and doubt what God has purposed for your life.

You have the ability to change your personal corner of the world around. In your mouth is the power to bring about such drastic changes that the world won't even know what hit it! You have the power!

*And this is the confidence that we have in Him, that if we **ask** any thing according to His will, He heareth us: and if we know that He hear us, whatsoever we **ask**, we know that we have the petitions that we desired of Him. (I John 5:14 – 15)*

***Ask** and it shall be given you... For everyone that **asketh** receiveth... (Matthew 7:7)*

Ask – to use words in seeking the answer to a question. To request; solicit. (Webster's New World Dictionary)

God is not on an ego trip and you are not a puppet on a string. Yes, God can read your mind; He is spirit. He can tell you the very next thought you are going to have. He can answer your question before you ask it. But...

He wants you to ask. He wants you to make your request known to Him through words.

"Well, God knows my heart."

There are two problems with this statement that I want to point out: it's pious and it's true. God does know our hearts. He knows the wickedness; He knows the perversity; He knows the hardness of our hearts. God knows how hard we work to cover up sin in our hearts by being super religious and so Heavenly-minded we are no Earthly good. He's not interested in that stuff. He wants to know the sincerity of our hearts.

"Well, God is omnipotent, omniscient, and omnipresent. I don't have to say a word and He will do it!"

God is all that and more. But, He desires that we ask for the things we need, want and desire in our lives. There is power in our words.

When we speak, we change the course of the universe. The power of our words transforms any negative situation we find ourselves in to one more favorable for us. Our words have the ability to create an atmosphere around us that is more productive for God's perfect will to be accomplished in our lives.

It's a spiritual thing. Just like God, our words are spirit. Our words occupy an entirely different dimension than what we can see with our naked eyes. Our words have such great power, they can do more than we could ever imagine.

Think about this:

"Mommie, I'm scared. There's a monster in my closet."

"Well, Baby, let's take care of that right now! Mr. Monster, I command you to come out of that closet right now and leave my baby alone!"

Once the mother makes that statement and the child hears it, the child is assured that the Closet Monster is gone. That precious little boy or girl can go to sleep with no other problems during the night. Now, let's look at this from a Christian perspective.

"Mr. Carson, if we don't receive a mortgage payment from you by August 1, we will proceed with foreclosure on your home that your family has been in for 25 years. We're sorry; there is nothing more we can do for you."

The above scenario takes place practically every day of the week. How the person who receives such a declaration chooses to process that statement in his or her heart makes all the difference in the world to their quality of life.

Now, Mr. Carson (fictitious name) has an opportunity that can be used positively or negatively. He can choose to bring life to his situation by his choice of words. Or, he can bring death. Let's see what he chooses to do.

*Verily I say to you, Whatsoever ye shall bind on earth shall be bound in heaven: and whatsoever ye shall loose on earth shall be loosed in heaven. Again I say unto you, That if two of you shall agree on earth as touching any thing that they shall **ask**, it shall be done for them of my Father which is in heaven. For where two or three are gathered together in my name, there am I in the midst of them. (Matthew 18:18 – 20)*

Mr. Carson and his family have been in their home for over 20 years. Needless to say, he and his family have grown attached to their home and many memories have come about in their hearts and lives since they have lived there.

Their children have grown up and gone out and started families of their own. Mr. and Mrs. Carson have seen other children, their neighbors, grow up and start families of their own. The Carson family loves their home and their neighborhood.

Unfortunately, the economy has not been kind. Life has thrown some curveballs at them. Mrs. Carson got sick and had to quit work. Mr. Carson's job cut his hours because they were losing business. Mr. Carson has worked part-time jobs but nothing has helped. And now a foreclosure!

Death and life are in the power of the tongue…

The Carson's discuss their situation. They decide to put all their trust in God. God has seen them through all these years. He has never left them and they know that He keeps His promises!

"Father, we thank you for the many years You have given us in our home. We thank You for allowing us to raise our family here and to see the things You have allowed us to see in these 25 years. Thank You, Lord, for sustaining us all these years. Now, Father, the mortgage company has told us we are about to lose our home. Father, we know that only Your Word will stand in this situation. We have decided to not take their decision lying down. We believe Your Word that whatever we bind on the earth is bound in heaven and what we loose on the earth is loosed in heaven. Right now, Father God, we bind foreclosure and lack over our situation. We recognize that there is no lack in Heaven. We bind foreclosure and lack in our lives on the earth and we know that it is bound in Heaven from affecting us. And Father God, we loose restoration and plenty in our lives on the earth because we are assured that restoration and plenty is loosed on our lives in Heaven. Nevertheless, Father, we also know that all things are working together for our good and for Your glory. Let Your Kingdom come and Your Will be done, on the earth as it is in Heaven! We thank You God that Your perfect will is being accomplished in our lives right now in the sweet Name of Jesus we pray! Amen!"

Did you know that God receives joy when His people pray in this way to Him? He is ecstatic when His people take Him at His Word and begin to war for the things He has already said belongs to them.

In the case of the Carson family, foreclosure was not something God had written about for them in the Book of Life. There are no foreclosures in Heaven; therefore, there should be no foreclosure on the Earth in the lives of those called by His name. God knew what was going on in this situation. He needed for this husband and wife to come before Him and earnestly pray for His perfect solution for them. God needed for Mr. and Mrs. Carson to come together in agreement for their beloved home.

But, notice how the Carson's prayed for God's Kingdom and His Will to come to them from Heaven. In any given situation, we have to seek God for **His** will to be done in our lives. When we do this, God receives the power He needs to effect the changes in our lives that need to come about because we have submitted all things to Him.

Now, God *can* and *will* use such devastating things as foreclosures. He uses tragic situations to cause us to move into the next phase or season in our lives He has planned for us. God uses anything and every situation. Nothing is wasted with God; He uses all things for His glory.

When God created the Heaven and the Earth, He spoke His creative power forth and things began to happen.

Let there be... (Genesis 1:3)

And there was! Light *became* and dispelled dark. The Earth, moon, sun, stars, and heavens *became* substance and dispelled the void of the universe. Seeds *became* and began to grow so that the planet we now call home thrives and flourishes as though involuntarily. But, we know the real reason why everything we see is here... **God said it!**

In I John 5:14 - 15, we are urged to ask by the will of God. If we do that, we can be assured that whatever we have asked for will be done for us. Let's go a bit deeper with that concept.

The passage begins, *And this is the confidence...*

Confidence loosely means to feel certain or assured. As we observed with the Carson's, we have to step boldly before the King of

Kings so that we can be assured of receiving what we request. We must have confidence in our relationship with God. If we have confidence in our relationship, we are assured that we are His children. We also must be convinced that He wants to give His very best to us.

Now, we can't come before God with a wimp-like faith: we won't receive anything! Although He could go ahead and do what we request, what would we learn? How would we grow? How would we obtain the faith we need for the next, more difficult request?

God knows this. He desires that we grow and mature in Him so that when we reach the difficulties of life, we can practically breeze right through them.

And this is the confidence that we have in Him…

Peter knew who Jesus was. He was very bold and outspoken when Jesus asked him who he said Jesus was.

Thou art the Christ, the Son of the Living God… (Mark 8:29)

Jesus applauded Peter for his boldness. Jesus knew that Peter did not receive that from just observing him. Jesus knew that Peter had gained that knowledge from the Spirit of God. He knew that Peter had grown confident in his knowledge. Jesus knew that, even though Peter stumbled at times, He could count on him to carry out the mission He would die to give to him.

Now, it's your turn. Do you have confidence in the Man Jesus? Do you have confidence that, even before you ask the question, He has already answered for your good and for His glory?

As you run on the Cross-Country Track of Life, do you *know* that you *know* that you *know* that God, through Jesus Christ, is working all things together for His glory and your good?

These are some of the issues you may need to get straight with yourself before you can move further with that scripture and receive the promise.

That if we ask any thing... Let's address this.

Any *thing...*

Lord, please help me to run faster on this Track.

Lord, please help me to pass this person in front of me.

Lord, please help me to catch my breath.

Lord, please help me to make $1,000 so I can pay my bills.

Lord, please make a full scholarship available for me so I can go to college and become an attorney.

Is there any difference in any of those questions? Each is asking a specific thing from God. ...To run faster; to pass someone; to catch my breath; to receive $1,000; to receive a scholarship. There is no difference in any of the questions being put before the Lord. The only difference is... your attitude.

The same way God answers your plea for strength is the same way He answers your cry for money. There is no difference with God.

"It seems to be more difficult for God to get money through to me."

Maybe God has something different planned. Once you release the "ask," He releases the answer. You don't ask and then tell God how you want the answer to come. You release the request to Him and know that His answer will be the best answer for you and for your situation. Just expect the answer to come.

Remember; we are on the Cross-Country Track of Life. On this Track, we encounter things that could possibly hinder our reaching the destination God has created for us. While we are being hindered, we have to cry out to God for assistance.

He already knows what we are coming up against. But, He wants us to vocalize it to Him. He wants us to hear ourselves asking for what we need from Him. Remember: *faith cometh by hearing...*

I want you to try something. Read I John 5:14 – 15. Just read it. Don't read it out loud; just read it in your mind. Now, read it out loud. Can you tell the difference?

When you read it silently, it was just something you read, wasn't it? You know, the words that you read meant something, but there was really not much power behind what you read. But, when you **heard** the words forming in your mouth and vibrating in your throat as you caught what you were saying with your ears, I can guarantee something different happened in your heart. You gained faith just by hearing the words instead of merely reading them.

As we hear the Word of God coming out of our mouths, our faith grows in our hearts and minds. We know, beyond a shadow of a doubt, that He will perform what we have asked.

According to His will...

Do you know God's will for your life? Have you asked Him what His will is for your life? How do you find His will for your life? How do you pray according to His will? Look at the Carson's prayer.

Thy Kingdom come, Thy WILL be done... (Matthew 6:10)

When the disciples asked Jesus to teach them to pray, He taught them what has become known as The Lord's Prayer. He taught them that after we give reverence to God, we submit everything we are and that we could hope to be to Him by giving everything back to Him.

When we ask that God's Kingdom come down from Heaven and manifest in our lives on the earth, God is then given the authority He needs to allow His greatest to come to pass in our lives.

When we pray *Thy Kingdom Come, Thy Will Be Done,* we are in reality saying, "God, although this is what I want to occur in my life, I know that what You desire for me is far better and greater than anything I could ever hope for. Let Your will be done."

And God will speedily answer the cry set before Him because you have verbalized and submitted everything to Him.

The more you use your words to touch God's heart, the more you will come to realize that your words have power with God. Those same words have power to create what you are crying out to God for. Also remember that the scripture assures us that if we ask, He will hear. God hears you!

He Hears You!

Out of the billions of voices in the Universe, **God Hears You!** Your voice is not insignificant. You voice is not unimportant. Let me repeat:

GOD...

HEARS...

YOU!

Things may seem to be going crazy... Or, crazier!

You might feel you are a magnet for chaos. But, pay attention! *You can't afford to get distracted!*

This is the reality: the greatest help we will ever receive will **always** come from the Father. So, we must make it our business to keep praying *to Him*. Keep talking *to Him*. He hears you.

Don't ever let the distractions of chaos and confusion over-power your time of prayer. God is **not** the Author of Confusion! Prayer is your greatest defense. I don't care how clichéd it may sound; prayer is still your *lifeline* toward getting out of your mess.

And I want you to think about something else. Every time you experience interruptions or distractions when you are trying to pray, it is the enemy of your soul. He does not want you to be able to pray.

He wants to take that gift from you so you can continue to live a defeated life.

Our adversary, the enemy of our souls, understands that the more he can create confusion and distractions in our lives, the least likely we are to pursue God through prayer. He will throw as much chaos and as many diversions our way as he can in an attempt to sidetrack us from our purpose.

We have to be careful. Sometimes we think we aren't saying the right words or praying in the correct manner. Believe it or not, satan can cause you to believe that your prayers aren't effective because you don't use $100 words every time you approach God. That's simply not true!

So what if we don't pray the most elaborate prayers or utter the holiest words? God is not looking for elaborate prayers. He wants sincere; He wants desire; He wants heart-felt. That's all. We may even feel unworthy to pray about our mess. That's OK, too.

If that's how you feel about praying and inviting God to get involved, then I want you to always remember Matthew 11:28-30:

Come to Me, all you who labor and are heavy laden, and I will give you rest. Take My yoke upon you and learn from Me, for I am gentle and lowly in heart, and you will find rest for your souls. For My yoke is easy and My burden is light.

Notice that the invitation is to **ALL**. All who labor (are engaged in the cares and problems of this life.) All who are heavy laden (with the cares and problems of this life that tend to weigh us down.)

Jesus didn't issue this invitation to those who could pray elaborate mixtures of words gaining His full attention. He didn't call on those who could pray the Heavens down and shake the earth.

He called for **ALL** who were weary; **ALL** who needed changes to occur in their situations. He promises to give us rest from those situations; a rest that allows us to concentrate on what's important: Him and our relationship with Him.

Jesus never leaves us feeling burdened. He never puts more on us than we can handle. (Frightening, isn't it, since we don't know exactly how much we **can** handle!)

When we go through the trials of life, we have to be confident that His strength is made perfect in our weakness. We have to have faith that He makes up the difference. You see, we work at a deficit; we never have enough as long as we work in our own power.

You would not place an ox with a mule to pull a load. For one thing, the mule would refuse to perform. Additionally, since the mule is weaker than the ox, the pairing would make it seem as though the ox has become as weak as the mule because the ox would not work to its full capacity. Their partnership is incompatible.

In our lives, we find that we have to work with the Lord in all things. For all intents and purposes, our partnership or work union with Jesus is incompatible. Our strength, compared to His, is very small. To the carnal or natural mind, we have nothing to offer to this relationship.

But, when we work with Him, submitting ourselves to Him, He carries us. As He carries us, we gain more strength. As we gain more strength, we are able to accomplish more. We become more confident to carry out our mission and work side-by-side with Him.

Be strong in the Lord and in the power of His might... (Ephesians 6:10)

We must acknowledge that everything we do is only accomplished by the power of God's might within us. Once we gain more strength, we should not allow pride and self-confidence to shield us from the fact that we need to decrease so that He can increase in our life and situation! As we decrease, more and more of His character is revealed in our lives. When this happens, others see Jesus in us and desire to be more like Him.

We have to continue coming to Him! The worse our problems become, the more we must elevate our minds and expand our conversations with Him. What do I mean exactly?

The enemy of your soul is very experienced in using distractive strategies. While keeping you from praying, these strategies also prevent you from raising your mind to where you need to focus your attention. He is capable of throwing situations at you that momentarily cause you to focus on the situation and not on God.

The Psalmist wrote, *I will lift up mine eyes unto the hills, from whence cometh my help. My help cometh from the Lord... (Psalms 121:1 – 2)*

Ultimately, all the help we will ever need comes from above. Yes, some people here on the earth may assist us out of our dilemma. However, God is the One Who equips our Earthly helpers to provide us with what we need.

Unfortunately, some of those same "helpers" are double agents who seem to work for both sides. On the one hand, the person seems to be a helper and encourager to us. On the other hand, the same person seems to create the trouble we find ourselves in.

Mess, drama, confusion, and sin, are huge distractions. That's typically what they're designed to do: distract. Our adversary attacks us in many different ways; he always seeks to bring distraction to our lives. But nothing, **NOTHING,** is more important than our fellowship with the Lord.

Even through the distractions, we have to teach ourselves to push in, to persevere or endure through prayer. In doing so, we teach ourselves to stand firmly on the ground God has placed us on.

And having done all, to stand. Stand therefore… (Ephesians 6:13b – 14a)

When we become confident that God hears our voice, our tiny voice, we have the confidence to stand in spite of all we may endure. Now is the time to remove all the distractions that hinder our prayer time. Once we remove the distractions, it becomes easier to hear from God. We are able to discern His voice more clearly.

Jesus understood the need for prayer. Take a look at the life of Christ in the book of Mark. Notice that even Jesus Himself had a powerful prayer life!

His followers did not understand the importance of prayer at the onset of His ministry. After watching Jesus flow in his anointing, though, they understood. They discovered that He received both instructions from God and the anointing through His prayer life. They ultimately discovered that God heard Jesus.

And so, they asked Jesus to teach them how to pray. This is a perfect example of how prayer not only changes us personally, but also the lives of those around us.

Many Christians are saved but actively engaged in sin. Knowledge of our imperfections has created a mental wedge between us, our prayer life, and our faith. The feelings of unworthiness we have can sometimes pose as a distraction that hinders us from pressing on toward becoming better Christians.

But faith and salvation go hand in hand. Apostle Paul puts it best in Ephesians 2:1-13:

And you were dead in your trespasses and sins, in which you formerly walked according to the course of this world . . . . But God, being rich in mercy, because of His great love with which He loved us, even when we were dead in our transgressions, made us alive together with Christ . . . . For by grace you have been saved through faith; and that not of yourselves, it is the gift of God; not as a result of works, that no one should boast. For we are His workmanship, created in Christ Jesus for good works, which God prepared beforehand, that we should walk in them . . . . But now in Christ Jesus you who formerly were far off have been brought near by the blood of Christ.

Wow! God is indeed awesome!

Make sure that you thank God daily for your salvation! Not only that, but thank Him for His grace!

In fact, according to Strong's Concordance, "grace" and "favor" in the New Testament (KJV) are always a translation of the Greek word, "charis" (khar'ece). Strong's Greek Lexicon defines it as "graciousness . . . of manner or act." The dictionary (Merriam-Webster Online) tells us "grace" is "unmerited divine assistance given man for his regeneration or sanctification."

So grace is favor, unmerited favor from the Lord. You can't earn His grace. His grace is given freely and abounds, even for you.

Before we close this section out, let's look at I John 5:14 – 15 again.

And this is the confidence that we have in Him, that if we ask any thing according to His will, He heareth us: and if we know that He hear us, whatsoever we ask, we know that we have the petitions that we desired of Him.

God hears you! He has and always will hear you. According to His will; according to His Word, He hears you. When He hears you, He does something.

SOMETHING!

He will not leave you hanging. He will not sit on His throne to see how crazy you look when you ask the same thing over and over and over… He's not that kind of God.

He is God Almighty. He is working all things out for your good and His glory! Trust Him. Believe in Him!

HE HEARS YOU!

The "H" Word

But He giveth more grace. Wherefore He saith, God resisteth the proud, but giveth grace unto the humble. Submit yourselves therefore to God. Resist the devil, and he will flee from you. (James 4:6 – 7)

Humble yourselves therefore under the mighty hand of God, that He may exalt you in due time… (I Peter 5:6)

There's something you need to know before we go any further: God has a problem with pride. You see, during the season in which He created the Heavens and the Earth, the Universe, He just happened to create a being who allowed his pride to pervert everything he was about.

This creature decided he would be better than God. This creature saw no reason why he wouldn't be able to take God's place one day as the Master of the Universe. He did everything in his power to thwart God at every turn.

He turned Adam and Eve from their true purpose to one of deceit and spiritual blindness. He tricked one-third of the heavenly host into following him into a life of darkness and sin. He caused untold numbers to follow him so he could get back at God.

To this day, this fallen angel continues to allow his pride to cause him to bump heads with God so he can have his way.

That will never happen!

You see, God gives grace to the humble; not the prideful. Look at Jesus.

Because Jesus humbly went to the Cross at Calvary, God raised Him up and gave Him a name that is above every name. Because of the blood that Jesus Christ shed on Calvary, that same blood has the power to cure, heal and deliver. Because of the beating Jesus humbly received prior to going to the cross, we **ARE** healed!

Isn't that awesome?

Think about it: Before He made His appearance on the Earth as our Savior, Jesus was a member of the Divine Trio Who created the universe. As a matter of fact, *in Him dwelleth all the fullness of the Godhead bodily, and ye are complete in Him, which is the head of all principality and power... (Colossians 2:9 – 10)*

Jesus was the physical representation of God the Father and God the Holy Spirit. He was and is the head of all principality and power. While enduring His trial, the Heavenly Hosts waited for Jesus to order them to come and do His will.

During his beating, Jesus could have had any number of Warrior Angels come to His rescue to smite the heads of His enemies. He could have called down a holy fire from the Heavens to wipe out those who would oppose Him. But, He didn't. Why?

Because *He was wounded for our transgressions, He was bruised for our iniquities, the chastisement of our peace was upon Him... (Isaiah 53:5)*

Jesus knew His role in the salvation of the world. He understood that one day you would pick up this book and read it. He knew that because of His trials, when you read this book, your faith could be built to the next level. He knew that one day you would go through what you are going through right now. He did what He did so you could make it through.

And so, He humbled Himself. Jesus, God in the flesh, became a scapegoat for you. He knew that your faith, at some point in your life, would become weak.

He humbled Himself so that He would be an example for you.

Humility is not easy and other people can and will make it hard for you to humble yourself. You will be told that you are weak. Someone will try to convince you that you are stupid. Someone else will tell you that you need to man- or woman-up. You will be told to stop being a wuss!

God is not concerned with any of these things because they are all unproven.

God says that when you are weak, He will be strong inside of you. He says that it is wise to fear Him. He says that in His Kingdom, there is neither male nor female, if you catch my drift. We are all the same in His Kingdom: His children.

So, since we are His children, it's all right to be humble under His hand. It's all right to just give it all to Him and let Him figure it out for you. Jesus did.

Nevertheless, not My will but Thy will… (Luke 22:42)

That's humility in its highest form. Honestly, to call on God and say, "Lord, this is what I want. But, Lord, let Your will be done in my life," takes more courage than going out and trying to figure things out for yourself. Submitting your life to God and fully committing to letting His perfect will be performed in your situation takes more nerve than coming up with your own solution.

God can work with that. He can take the nothing out of your situation and, because you have asked for His will to be done, make something out of it.

Now, let's consider one of the passages of scripture from the beginning of this section.

But He giveth more grace. Wherefore He saith, God resisteth the proud, but giveth grace unto the humble. (James 4:6 – 7)

The situation you are facing right now could use some grace. You need grace to make it through. You need grace to give you wisdom. You need grace to show you the solution.

God supplies that grace to you; **but**, only if you humble yourself to Him. How do you do that? Let's find out through Jonah.

Jonah hated Nineveh! He hated the people, he hated what they stood for; he hated their very souls. They had treated Israel and tortured his people so badly, he wanted nothing to do with them.

God gave Jonah an assignment. He wanted Jonah to go to Nineveh and preach eight words: *"Yet forty days, and Nineveh shall be overthrown." (Jonah 3:4)*

That's all; nothing more, nothing less. He didn't tell Jonah to go in and hold a tent revival. He didn't tell him to have a camp meeting.

"Yet forty days, and Nineveh shall be overthrown."

But, Jonah didn't want the assignment. He knew exactly what God was going to do: save Nineveh and her people. He didn't *want* them to be saved. He wanted them to perish and go to… Well, you know where he wanted them to go.

So, he turned down the assignment; or, so he thought he did. He decided to go on vacation!

Jonah chose to go on a cruise to Tarshish. He packed his bag, paid his fare, got on the ship, went down to his stateroom and went to sleep. Surely there he would be away from the presence of the Lord!

God resisteth the proud…

It wasn't too long after Jonah boarded the ship that havoc broke out on the seas. The ship and all its occupants were tossed to and fro, hither and yon as the sea pitched. A great wind arrested the ship crew's efforts to make it to their destination. They were very afraid. They had no idea what was going on. Jonah slept!

The mariners tried every measure they could think of to avoid the coming disaster. They threw freight overboard to lighten the load. Nothing. They cried to their gods. Nothing.

Finally, the shipmaster came to his senses. He saw that his gods weren't working. He decided to see if there was another God Who would. He went down to Jonah's berth and woke him up. He read him the riot act because he and his crew were going crazy just to stay alive.

Of course, Jonah knew what was going on. He told them who he was and how he was running away from the mission God had assigned to him. But, you need to know that Jonah had grace for this situation.

Yes, he messed up. Yes, he was disobedient to the Lord. But, God still placed grace on Jonah's life.

As soon as Jonah told the crew the solution and they followed through, everything calmed down for them as though nothing had happened. But, look at God's grace through this: the mariners praised the true God because they saw His mighty works! Through Jonah's disobedience, God was able to show Himself to be more powerful than the gods they prayed to.

God's grace was in full operation even during Jonah's disobedience! You see, even in his pride, Jonah showed a certain amount of humility. Instead of boldly standing on the deck in the face of destruction, he attempted to hide himself from the face of the Lord. He knew God was there!

When Jonah was thrown overboard, a big fish came and scooped him up. Now, the Lord could have destroyed Jonah but He had a plan. The grace He wanted to extend to the people of Nineveh was upon Jonah. God's plans would not be frustrated!

God has given you an assignment. Unlike Jonah, you want to complete the assignment but you are afraid: of the unknown; of what others may say; of failure.

There are numerous reasons you might be afraid. But, know this: **God's grace is upon you!** He is waiting for you to submit these emotions to Him. He is waiting for you to humble yourself under His mighty hand so He can exalt you when the time comes.

God is not interested in failure, but, He can use failure for His purposes as well. He is, however, very interested in your success. He will allow you to take all the time in the world because He has designed the timeline just for you; just as He did with Jonah.

He is waiting for you to come to the end of yourself. In faith and with humility, He wants you to ask Him to help you move forward so you can complete the assignment He has given to you. The mission He has designed for you is not just for you to help and assist other people. God's mission is also to help you become more mature in Him so that you will be more effective in future missions. Rest assured: there will be future missions!

As we have seen with Jonah, God will not allow us to run away from our assignment. He allows us to get on the ship; He even makes arrangements for us to get the best stateroom onboard. However, at some point, while the ship is tossing to and fro, the crew will discover us and we will have our reckoning moment with God.

And, yes, our faith will be tried. God's methods are beyond our limited understanding. He will ask us to do things and we will have no idea **what** the outcome will be. He will allow us to sail on the Sea of Change just so we can come out into the place He has for us.

God will encourage us to go forward with the plan even when we don't agree with the plan. He will encourage us to succeed but He will not enable us to make excuses. Let's move forward.

God Encourages and Enables

Give a man a fish you feed him for one day. Teach him how to fish you feed him for a lifetime. ~Author Unknown~

There is a purpose for your reading this book. You have come to a point in your life in which you need faith and, probably, a lot of it. You have been able to, more or less, live off your parent's faith until this point in your life. Now, though, you find that you have to believe God for yourself.

You probably don't remember, but, your life changed drastically when you learned to walk. From the time you first began to gain independence, you found that you liked independence and craved more of it.

Ideally, while in the learning stages, your parents assisted you as much as they could. At the beginning, either your mom or dad or both were there to catch you every time you stumbled. If you fell to the floor, they were there to pick you up, dry your tears, and put you back down so you could continue to discover the ins and outs of walking.

Once you got the hang of it, you wanted no parts of their hands on your small, tottering body. You waddled from room to room, place to place, in search of new adventures as your walking became running. You never stopped! And you have been moving forward ever since.

When you finally entered the hallowed halls of pre-school, you experienced another burst of freedom and began to accumulate new friends and confidantes. During this season, you began to leave your parent(s) behind. They reluctantly gave you some play in the reins of life that held you near and dear to their hearts.

You may have been allowed to participate in overnights or sleepovers by the time you became 10, maybe 9. You relished being able to be with your friends and not around your parents!

Everything that needed to come into your life, your parents believed for. They didn't bother you with their hopes and dreams for you and themselves. They believed God, had faith that He would come through for them, for you, and their other children. Many of the things you received in life, not just food and shelter, but those things you may have taken for granted, those things that seemed to appear at your every whim, came because your parents activated *their* faith muscles. They built on their faith and strengthened their faith because they wanted you to have those things. They wanted the best for their little one.

As time passes according to the time of life, however, you have to believe for yourself. Yes, you are probably still under their care; you still have basic needs that they can and will take care of. But, you also want other things.

You want to be the star of the class play.

You want to be on the first-string for football, basketball, soccer, or tennis.

You want to go out with the Captain of the Cheerleading squad.

You want to get all A's so you can get a scholarship to the college of your choice.

You want to get that job with that multi-millionaire dollar corporation and work your way to the upper ranks.

These are **your** hopes, dreams and desires. These activities make **your** heart beat faster. Being assigned the starring role in the school play takes **your** breath away at the possibility of getting what you desire. Therefore, **you** have to have faith.

You have to have faith that what you have asked for from God for your life will be accomplished because it is His will to give it to you. You prayed for that bicycle when you were 9; it was God's will for you to have it and He gave it to you through your parents.

Do you have faith to believe for what you want in your life? What is that one thing God has placed in your heart and that you know is for you? What do you want? What is your main reason for reading this book and learning about faith? What do you believe that God will do in your life?

David was a teen when the Prophet Samuel came to anoint him as King. David had realized from a young age that something was different about his life.

He was in charge of his dad's flock of sheep when he had to protect those little babies with his very life by slaying both a lion and a bear. Only great people could do things like that. But, that didn't make him a king, did it?

When Samuel came to David's father, Jesse's, house, David was out in the field doing his usual; tending the flock. Samuel commanded Jesse to bring all his sons to a feast so that he could anoint one of them to be the King of Israel. (I Samuel 16)

Jesse brought out his sons, starting with the eldest, one by one.

"Here's Eliab, the oldest…" Jesse offered to the Man of God.

"No, he's not the one," God said to Samuel.

" OK, then, here's Abinadab…"

"Nope. Not that one either."

Seven times this exchange took place. Both Samuel and Jesse were perplexed. Jesse had presented his sons; the best of the best. Surely…

"Jesse, do you have any more sons?" Samuel asked, probably wondering what the Lord was up to.

"Well, I do have one more; the youngest, David. He's out in the field with the sheep. But, he's just a little thing. A scrawny kid," Jesse protested to the Prophet.

"Bring him. We will not sit down until I see **that** one."

God had already told Samuel not to look at how tall the person was or how good he looked. When it comes to fulfilling a destiny, looks and height don't matter to God. God wants the heart.

He is looking at your heart right now. He knows you are a lion waiting to be loosed. He knows you have the heart of a king because He equipped you with the heart of a king.

As soon as Samuel saw David, his heart quickened. He realized in that instance that his eyes were gazing upon the King of Israel; God's chosen king.

Then Samuel took the horn of oil, and anointed him in the midst of his brethren: and the Spirit of the Lord came upon David from that day forward. (I Samuel 16:13)

Now, at this point, David could have had a shout fest: he was the next King of Israel! But, he didn't. David had to go back to work tending the sheep!

What?

David was chosen for the position of King but his appointment was a little ways off. God had to set some things straight before He would allow David to sit in that office.

Many times, we feel that God is off in the way He does things. He is not. We pray and we pray and we pray. We walk the walk and talk the talk of faith. We believe, cry, pray, and then believe some more.

We become discouraged because everything seems to move so slowly. We lose faith.

Then, something positive happens and our faith is renewed. We find a little strength and build a little more faith. We hear a testimony from another saint and discover we can believe a little more. God has sent encouragement through the Pastor. We can make it!

Then, the bottom falls out and we go through the cycle again. But, let's back up to the encouragement God sent.

Consider David. Once he was anointed as the new King of Israel, God brought changes into his life. When he went to the Army campsite to see how his brothers were doing, God opened a door for David to become the champion of his people. This brought him in front of the reigning king, Saul.

Once recognized as the champion of the people of Israel, though, King Saul wanted to kill David. Saul recognized that this young man had something he didn't have. After all, David killed Goliath. Saul knew that David would probably end up being the King of Israel.

Eventually, Saul did discover that David had been anointed king; he had to get rid of him. Never mind Saul had been disobedient to the commandment of the Lord; never mind he had failed to completely do what God called him to do. No; he had to rid himself of David because he was the king and no one was going to take that away from him!

David was forced to hide in caves! He had to play crazy in order to receive asylum with one of the enemy kingdoms! He had to patiently wait out the doings of God so he would obtain the promise.

Cast not away therefore your confidence, which hath great recompence of reward. For ye have need of patience, that, after ye have done the will of God, ye might receive the promise. For yet a little while, and he that shall come will come, and will not tarry. (Hebrews 10:35 – 37)

God wants you to have what He has promised to you. Just as with David, God has anointed you with something and sent you back to the sheep field. You have had to battle it out with the lions and bears of life. You have had to hide from your enemies in the caves of frustration. You have even had to play crazy so that no one could tell who and what you really are.

Nevertheless, God has encouraged you time and time again! He has enabled you to make it! He has put that *something* down in your spirit that causes you to keep moving forward! And guess what? You are!

You are moving forward! You experience success after success! You see more and more of what God has for you. You have even determined what God wants from you and you are doing it.

Your relationship with God becomes stronger and stronger. You now see Him moving obstacles out of your way that previously hindered you. You discover that abundant favor is upon you and you can do things you could not do in the past. God is enriching your life with experiences and people you had only dreamed about before.

You experience open doors that were closed to you before. You hear the resounding thud of doors closing that were open before. You actually **know** which door to go through now because God has *enabled* you to know. Now, you don't waste time going through dead-end doors; you only walk through the doors that are vital for what God has for you.

God desires to be an encourager as well as an enabler in your life. He wants you to experience the positives of both these traits so you can become an encourager as well as an enabler in someone else's life.

When Saul first met David, he loved him. He called him son. Saul fed David at his own table. When he found out what David could do, he wanted no more to do with David. He wanted him dead. Saul even used his own daughter as a foil to kill David. Fortunately, David had a relationship with God that caused him to be very aware of the things Saul tried to do.

As David sat in the cave, he could have been discouraged. He could have pouted, selfishly reminding God about some things he felt should have taken place already.

"You *said* I would be king! Why do I have to live in this cave?"

"Why don't You just kill Saul and be done with it? I am Your chosen one, aren't I?"

But, David **humbled** himself before God. (Yes, there's that word again.) He knew God had a plan. David knew he had to do what he needed to do and God would do what He said He would do.

While in the cave, David grew his army. Those people who were in distress, in debt, or discontent joined David in the cave named Adullam and became a part of his army. His parents, whose lives were probably in danger because of Saul, even joined David in the cave.

At the same time, David's confidence in the Lord grew. As his confidence grew, David learned to encourage himself. A direct result of the encouragement he gave to himself was shown in his ability to move forward into the destiny God had created for him.

Look at the Book of Psalms. It is said that of the 150 Psalms gathered in the Bible, David was the author of at least 75 of them. In those 75 Psalms, David pours out his very soul to God about his life and the situations he found himself in. As he created those Psalms, he found new levels of worship and appreciation for the God he found himself serving. As you read the Psalms, I am sure you will find the inspiration behind the theme of this book, *Even Me.*

I will bless the Lord at all times; His praise shall continually be in my mouth. My soul shall make her boast in the Lord: the humble shall hear thereof, and be glad. O magnify the Lord with me, and let us exalt His name together. (Psalms 34:1 – 3)

Regardless of the situation David found himself in, he always found something praiseworthy about the Lord. He moved in faith, encouraging and enabling himself to reach the heights that God wanted him to reach.

What about you? Are you considering the place you are in and finding it hard to encourage yourself to move forward? Do you find it hard to even believe that God has more for you than what you see?

Let God be you encourager and enabler. He has so much more for you and He wants you to fulfill the destiny He has designed for you. He will strengthen you and push you forward. He is faithful!

Make No Mistake; He Will Perform It

A few years ago, I remember waiting with anticipation to see this stage play I had heard about. Local television advertisements boasted that this play would be soulful, life-changing, and power-packed. According to the commercials, the show was jam-packed with stars, the music was stellar, and it was just going to be an awesome experience.

So, like many other people, I decided to make a sacrifice and purchased tickets to this play. As the date of the event drew nearer, I began to get my hopes up. I was so excited about this play! I began to hype friends and family about it; not because I'd seen the show, but because of what I'd heard from others' reports and the ads. After a while, just the anticipation of this trip to the theater had become a groundbreaking awakening, a "must-see" for me.

Finally, the day of the show arrived. There I was doing everything I could to prepare and make sure I looked and smelled my best only to learn, an hour before show time, that the performance had been cancelled! Wow, what a major disappointment! Suddenly, after all that time, and all that hype, my life-changing theater experience was not going to happen.

It was only a couple of years later that I began to have a powerful revelation about that whole experience. You see, God never says He will do something and not perform it. Whatever God has said He will do in your life, you can be certain that He will perform it!

Here we are believers of Christ. We have the Word as advertisement for the promises of God. These are promises we've been told about over and over again, through good times and bad. This is the instruction we need in our lives, the instruction God has given to us.

Many of us have been in church most of our lives. The same Word we have heard over and over again, preached while we were so small all we could do during the service was sleep on the pew, is the same word we now find relevant in our lives as teens and young adults.

We remember Sister Always B. Blessed. Sister Blessed got up and testified every Sunday about the good things God did in her life; things she wanted to happen but only happened as a result of her finding faith in God and believing in His Word. Her faith served as million dollar advertising of the goodness and faithfulness of God. It drew others to the altar because they wanted what they knew only God could perform in their lives.

We recall Brother Triple G (Give God Glory) getting up right after Sister Blessed. Brother G. would tell the congregation how God showed up and showed out at his job. He shared with us how God performed in opening up a door for him to receive a promotion. That promotion was supposed to go to someone who had a much better education than Brother G. But, because of God's faithfulness, reported Brother G., he received the promotion instead. His faith also served as a full front page advertisement that drew in people like wildfire to see the goodness of the Lord in action.

Sunday after Sunday, the word got around. The reports drew even more people who were excited about the goodness of the Lord and His faithfulness. As God performed greater and more awesome productions of His power for His people, those called by His name, by the power of the Holy Spirit, the Word drew in even more people!

As children, listening to these testimonies, we heard but did not hear this free advertising. Sunday after Sunday, we were hyped up on the Word of God by our parents. As we got older, we became more aware of the works of God in our lives as our parents believed for bigger and greater things.

In a way, we took it for granted because we knew that the things we saw, the blessings and miracles, were results of the faith our parents had in God. Then, it was our turn.

We had to start believing God for things to happen in our lives. We arrived at church for the testimonies. We began to see people our own age getting up to give their testimonies.

Young Brother Will B. Done got up and testified about God's perfect will being done in his life. He testified how he applied for a particular program and scholarship being given at a college three states over and receiving the scholarship, instead, for a different program. Young Brother Done didn't think he was eligible for the program but, look at how the Lord performed. Hallelujah!

Then, your best friend, Sister G. (To God Be Glory, Brother G's daughter,) gave her testimony. She has believed God for an internship as an assistant producer with the local cable television station in your hometown. Instead, God performed a miracle. The top news affiliate in your state, WKBN CBS news, saw her segment on a local event, contacted her, and asked if she would consider coming to work for them as one of the executive producers at the state affiliate in the capital. They want her to produce the political segments on their upcoming political broadcasts. This is far more than what Young Sister G and her family had expected! God showed up and showed out on her behalf as never before.

Unfortunately, many of us don't show any confidence or enthusiasm in what the Word says. We have the Word of God as our beacon; yet, we don't radiate as much confidence in His proven Word as we do in our overhyped media events. Instead of seeing a cancellation as merely a delay in God's perfect will being performed in our lives, we look at the cancellation only as that: a cancellation.

We think that God has cancelled what He said he would do. Not true.

Sometimes, God will delay an event in our lives because certain other things need to be accomplished first.

We may need a bit more maturity, for one. Other things may need to line up, for another. The recipient of the outcome may not be ready for the event to take place, for still another.

We never know what needs to be accomplished in our lives or the lives of others before God can perform what He says will be performed in our lives.

One of the greatest things we can do to encourage ourselves through our situation is begin to truly value God's Word and His promises. Just as I did with that show, we need to begin to build up those around us—friends, family, and strangers—with the wonderful Word of God.

Jesus says in Matthew 28:16-20 NIV, *All authority in heaven and on earth has been given to Me. Therefore go and make disciples of all nations, baptizing them in the name of the Father and of the Son and of the Holy Spirit, and teaching them to obey everything I have commanded you. And surely I am with you always, to the very end of the age.*

If you do what Jesus has commanded, let me tell you what happens to you on the days when you find yourself down and out. Because you have spoken and shared the Word of God, these individuals—

these witnesses— you have shared it with are able to take the Word of God you've sown into their lives and sow it back into your life! They are now equipped to lift **you** up while you're in the midst of your trouble!

You see, one thing is certain about the word of God: every promise He has made for you in your life **will come to pass.** He's not like that show I was so excited about seeing; He **will** show up. Make no mistake about it: **God will perform it.**

Constantly remind yourself of Isaiah 55:11, *So shall my word be that goeth forth out of my mouth: it shall not return unto me void, but it shall accomplish that which I please, and it shall prosper in the thing whereto I sent it.*

God will show up. Now, it may not seem that way outwardly. But, live with confidence, knowing that God will do just what He has said He will do. He is the main attraction and He really will show up, right on time. He sees you. And He's got you covered.

So, don't throw away your confidence for what God said He would do. He has never said something and not performed. He is always well able to do just what He says He will do. Sometimes, though, we have to wait patiently for the thing He has promised in our lives. We have to exercise this patience even though we don't want to exercise patience.

Patience is a fruit of the Spirit of God. The good fruit of the Spirit of God is firm and sweet and something we all should enjoy. God wants us to enjoy all the fruit He has given to us. So, let's open this piece of fruit in the next section so we can receive all that God has promised to us!

Be Patient

God has promised something to you; and, you want it! Your very core, your essence, is in deep, unmoving anticipation as you wait for what God has promised to you.

Everyone you associate with knows you are waiting for **something**. Their level of faith increases as you walk the walk and talk the talk of the faithful believer.

Every day, in every way, you breathe faith. You know God is good for what He has promised to you!

As time goes on, though, and you see nothing, you begin to waver. Your faith dips and dives as you wonder, "Did I really hear from God? Father, did I really hear your voice?"

Your friends and associates, your family, begin to question you about the thing God promised to you. You want to answer but you can't find the words to tell them. Even though you are still waiting for God to make His move, you can't seem to find that boost of confident assurance you need to keep you motivated.

You revisit everything you were told. You go back to the notes you wrote down when God revealed His plan for your life. You look at the date on the notes. So much time has passed!

Then, doubt comes.

"Did God really say…?"

"Why isn't it here yet?"

"What if I was wrong?"

"Is it really going to happen?"

Someone calls with a word of encouragement. The person assures you that you are doing what God has called you to do. You are told repeatedly to stand…

Having done all, to stand. Stand therefore… (Ephesians 6:13b, 14a)

Let's talk about *having done all* first. Having overcome all…

You have followed God to the best of your ability. You have done everything you were instructed to do. You have received, by faith, the direction the Holy Spirit has given to you. You have accepted the assignment for the Kingdom of God and courageously moved forward in the gifts and calling of God.

But, nothing has happened. As a matter of fact, it seems as though you are moving backward instead of forward. It seems as though every time you take one step forward, something, a situation or circumstance, seems to push you two to three steps backward! You don't understand.

You revamp your resume… Again.

You take a refresher course for your field… Again.

You network with some folks you previously worked with… Again.

You submit the application for that job online… Again.

You call Human Resources and spoke to the chief… Again.

You pray and fast… Again.

You call on the Prayer Warriors… Again.

You have the Pastor anoint you… Again.

Having done all…

What is there left for you to do?

Stand…

Stand – New World Dictionary of the American Language – 11. To maintain one's opinion, viewpoint, adherence, etc.; remain resolute or firm. 12. To make resistance, as to hostile action.

Did God tell you…

I will promote you on your job and you will receive more money and more responsibility!

You will get that new position because I have opened it up specifically for you!

You will be transferred to Detroit and become the youngest Manager in that position!

You will receive a full scholarship to Harvard, Yale, MIT!

God has spoken to your Spirit. You know His voice, but…

Stand therefore…

"Lord, I know what you told me. But it's getting harder and harder. When, Lord, When?"

You have just about given up, haven't you? Nothing has happened in so long, you doubt that anything is really going to happen.

Stop it! God is not finished yet!

It's **not** over! God said He **will** do it! You have to be convinced that what He has promised, He is able also to perform. You have to get this thought into your 'know-er.' You must reprogram your conscious to receive the knowledge that God has spoken and what He has spoken He will perform.

Hebrews 10:35 – 38a *Cast not away therefore your confidence, which hath great recompence of reward. For ye have need of patience, that, after ye have done the will of God, ye might receive the promise. For yet a little while, and he that shall come will come, and will not tarry. Now the just shall live by faith…*

To maintain one's opinion… Remain resolute… To make resistance.

The first thing we must expect when God gives a promise is that *opposition will come.* The enemy of our souls is set to counter everything God does in our lives. He will set up snares so that nothing of what God promises will reach us. And if it does reach us, the enemy, satan, the devil, will do whatever he can to delay or destroy what God has promised. He wants us to become discouraged. He wants to change our belief system around to his way of thinking: that what we have been promised will not come to pass.

The second thing we should expect is that the enemy of our souls will use whomever and whatever tactic he can to remove our faith and trust in God and the promises He has given to us. He will use family, friends, and associates to discourage us as much as he possibly can. He will take positive situations and fill them with negativity so that we will doubt what God has said to us.

While we are standing, waiting for the manifestation of the promise, we have to hone our "patience" skills. It will not be easy. Many of us have very few "patience" seeds in our lives as it is. The ones we do have, we tend to hoard instead of plant. We will have to fight to plant these patience seeds. We will have to resist the Birds of Deceit from coming and taking the very seed out of the ground! We can't give up!

Notice the advice we are given in Hebrews Chapter 10. **After** we do the will of God, we are to wait patiently for the promise of God. Sometimes, the promise immediately comes. Other times, which is probably the more common practice, the promise will take time to come.

While we wait, we can't cast aside or lose our confidence. We have to fight to maintain a high level of confidence in what God has promised to us. Our confidence has its own special reward: a reward that God will perform on our behalf and present us with the thing that has been promised to us.

We can't throw away our confidence in what God has spoken. We have to become more fierce in our confidence because therein lies the promise. We have to wait on Him knowing that what He has promised will come to pass.

God will come through! He always does.

Look at Abraham.

Hebrews 6:13 – 15 *For when God made promise to Abraham, because He could swear by no greater, He sware by Himself, saying, surely blessing I will bless thee, and multiplying I will multiply thee. And so, after he had **patiently** endured, he obtained the promise.*

God made a promise to Abraham. He promised this 80-something year-old man that He was going to provide him with an heir. This heir would come through his own loins from his barren 70-something year-old wife. Did alarm bells just sound off in your brain?

Let's see: 80-year old man and 70-year old woman. Something just doesn't sound right about that, especially considering Sarah was barren: her reproductive organs did not work!

Nevertheless, God made the promise to Abram (his name at the time.) Up until this point, God had been a promise keeper to Abram and his people. Abram had seen the Lord do many magnificent works in his life and the lives of his people. He had made a covenant with God and saw no reason to doubt God. But, a baby? Well…

And so, Abram patiently endured…

His wife came up with the idea that, since she was unable, she would provide a surrogate for her husband. (**Mind you: God didn't tell her to do this. She just felt the need to help out!**)

And so, Abram and Sarah conceived a child through Hagar. At the young, spry age of 86, Abram had his first-born: a son he named Ishmael.

But, you see, that's not what God promised. God promised that the heir, the promise, would come from Sarah's body.

Fast forward 13 years: Abram is now 99 and Sarah is 89. God changes their names to Abraham, Father of many nations, and Sarah, Princess. The next year, when Abraham became 100 and Sarah 90, Isaac, the promised heir, was born. God did what He said He would do.

At the proper time and in the proper atmosphere, God fulfilled His promise to Abraham and Sarah. He fulfilled His covenant with this old man because God needed certain things to be fulfilled in His created world.

Now, God has made promises to you. They may not be as outrageous as the promises He made to Abraham and Sarah. On the other hand, the promises He has made to you may be equally or more outrageous. You will also have to patiently endure the process so that you will receive the promise.

Come on! You can do it! Here's a laundry list to remember:

Stand therefore…

1. Put on the **Whole Armor of God** (Ephesians 6:10 – 18) and stand flat-footed and firm against the opposition that is sure to come. Stand, resolute in your faith, knowing that God will make good on the promises He has made to you.

2. **Renew your mind** (Romans 12:1 – 2) so that you will know God's good, and acceptable, and perfect will for your life. By the power of His Holy Spirit, He will reveal to you all the knowledge you need so that you can follow the path He has laid out for you.

3. **Keep your eyes lifted to the hills** (Psalms 121.) If you continue to look up to God where He sits on His Holy Hill, you will eventually disregard the stuff going on around you on this level. God desires that we constantly keep our focus on Him so that our thoughts are elevated to where all of our help really comes from.

4. **Invite Jesus In.** (Revelation 3:20 – 22) Jesus is knocking at the door of your heart. Will you let Him in? Will you allow Him to come in and make the changes in your life that need to be made so that the promise *can* come?

   Don't go anywhere; we are almost done.

He Only Needs An Invitation

Right now, at this very moment, many of us are finding ourselves in a place much like that of Abraham. In the book of James, Abraham is referred to as a 'friend' of God. He is a wonderful example of how we should do just what God says to do while we wait for the promise.

Abraham also had to run on the Cross Country Track of Life. He had to patiently endure and keep running while he waited for what God had promised to him and his wife. Without enduring patiently, Abraham might have experienced a delay of the greatness that God desired for his life. Had he not been willing to endure, he might have come off the Track and missed what God had for him. He could very well have stopped with Ishmael and not finished the course God had laid out for him.

God desires that you patiently endure for the promise He has made in your life. He does not desire any delays as He brings about the greatness He has prepared for your life. Now, it may seem impossible sometimes that the promises we have from God will **ever** come to pass. But, we can rest assured that they will come to pass.

So, the next time you're running the Cross Country Track of Life and are distracted from the will of God for your life, remember this: many have already been there; *even me.* You can adjust the lyrics for

the new revelation you will receive after reading this book. You can
sing:

Lord, I see the showers of blessing,

Thou art scattering full and free to me.

You shower my thirsty soul refreshing,

While Thou art blessing me.

Thank you, Lord, for blessing me.

Even me, Lord, Even me!

Even me, Oh Lord, Even Me.

You've let some drops now fall down on me.

Thank You, Lord, for blessing me.

There is another contemporary songwriter who penned an
outstanding song, in which he declared, *"You're next in line for your
miracle."*

Even you are next in line to receive what God has promised. But,
you must be confident and consistent in knowing that God will do
what He has said He will do. Stay faithful and prayer-ful; God is well
able to handle the rest.

Unlike Sarah, you should not feel you have to help God fulfill what
He has already destined for you. After all, He is God. He laid the
Earth's foundation a long time ago. He handcrafted the very heavens.
The Heavens will eventually wear out and become old like a used

garment. Yet, God will still be around when they're long gone. He will remain the same, and His years shall have no end.

Even if your mind can't fathom just how great our God is, know in your heart that He is. Even if your situation seems insurmountable, just know that He's greater. Allow Him to be Who He is to you without limits, without constraints. He is standing at the door knocking, but He will not intrude.

Revelation 3:20 says, *Here I am! I stand at the door and knock. If anyone hears My voice and opens the door, I will come in and eat with him, and he with Me.*

So, make certain that you extend a daily invitation to Him to feel welcome to enter your life. Let Him know continually that you are willing for Him to bring you to the place He has destined you to be.

When you have a moment, feel free to say the following prayer. It is my hope that this book has boosted your faith in some way and that it fills your spirit in a lasting way. God Bless!

Father, I thank You for this inspiration. Thank You, Lord, for this written boost toward being the very thing that You've called me to be. I thank You, Lord God, for making me steadfast, unmovable, and always abounding in Your work. I'm grateful, Lord, that You see what I cannot see, hear what I cannot hear, and feel what I cannot bear. I thank You, Lord, that the plans You have made for my life are perfect and true. Thank you, Lord, that adversity will not overwhelm or consume me in any way. I declare that, in my life, You will always be the head, and not the tail. Father, You shall forever reign over my destiny. Thank You for the stability in my walk with You, Lord God. Please give me the ability to continue to yield to Your will from this day forward. In the saving, redeeming name of Jesus, I pray. AMEN.

Promises Of God

* God has promised His people eternal life. (John 10:27, 28)

* He has promised to supply every need we have. (Philippians 4:19: But my God shall supply all your need according to his riches in glory by Christ Jesus.)

* God has promised that His grace is sufficient for us. (II Corinthians 12:9)

* God has promised that His children will not be overtaken with temptation. Instead, He assures us that a way of escape will be provided. (I Corinthians 10:13: No temptation has seized you except what is common to man. And God is faithful; he will not let you be tempted beyond what you can bear. But when you are tempted, he will also provide a way out so that you can stand up under it). And (Jude 1: 24: Now unto Him that is able to keep you from falling, and to present you faultless before the presence of his glory with exceeding joy.).

* God has promised that all things work together for the good of those who love and serve Him faithfully. (Romans 8:28)

* God has promised us victory over death. He first resurrected Jesus by way of assuring our resurrection. Paul wrote to the Corinthians (I Corinthians 15:3,4): For I delivered unto you first of all that which I

also received, how that Christ died for our sins according to the scriptures, and that he was buried, and that he rose again the third day according to the scriptures. Later on he adds (I Corinthians 15:57): But thanks be to God, which giveth us the victory through our Lord Jesus Christ.

* God has promised that those who believe in Jesus and are baptized for the forgiveness of sins will be saved. (Mark 16:16 and Acts 2:38)

About The Author

For more than a decade, Marc Raby's artistic gifts have served as dynamic ministering tools to a vast array of audiences. Marc is the author of several stage productions, including Love Shouldn't Hurt So Bad, Love and Insecurity, and Show Me Where It Hurts, just to name a few. He has made his mark as both a prolific writer and motivational speaker. He developed a passion for the arts at an early age, and he has been a singer, songwriter, dancer, and director.

Over the years, Marc decided to take the artistic skills with which he was gifted and turn them toward humanitarian efforts. He has aimed to display the vast greatness of God through many forms of entertainment and through his Christian faith. The cornerstone of his ministry is the declaration that, "As Long As God is In the Plans, Great Things Are Always in the Works."

Marc also founded AMRAE Ministries Inc., A Community Development Corporation, which aims to provide individuals with training in acting, speech, singing, playing musical instruments, and dance. Through such media, combined with scriptural doctrine, AMRAE Ministries Inc. promotes moral values, family enrichment, faith development, and social enlightenment (www.amraevision.com).

Even Me (Lord I Hear Of Showers Of Blessings)"

Words: Elizabeth Codner, 1860.

Music: William Bradbury, 1862.

"Lord, I hear of showers of blessing,

Thou art scattering full and free;

Showers the thirsty land refreshing;

Let some drops now fall on me;

Even me, even me,
Let some drops now fall on me.

Pass me not, O God, my Father,
Sinful though my heart may be;
Thou mightst leave me, but the rather;
Let Thy mercy light on me;
Even me, even me,
Let Thy mercy light on me.

Pass me not, O gracious Savior,
Let me live and cling to Thee;
I am longing for Thy favor;
Whilst Thou'rt calling, O call me;
Even me, even me,
Whilst Thou'rt calling, O call me.

Pass me not, O mighty Spirit!
Thou canst make the blind to see;
Witnesses of Jesus' merit,
Speak the Word of power to me;
Even me, even me,
Speak the Word of power to me.

Have I been in sin long sleeping,
Long been slighting, grieving Thee?
Has the world my heart been keeping?
O forgive and rescue me;
Even me, even me,
O forgive and rescue me.

Love of God, so pure and changeless,
Blood of Christ, so rich and free;
Grace of God, so strong and boundless
Magnify them all in me;
Even me, even me,
Magnify them all in me.

Pass me not; but pardon bringing,
Bind my heart, O Lord, to Thee;
Whilst the streams of life are springing,
Blessing others, O bless me;
Even me, even me,

Blessing others, O bless me.

Closing Gratitude

As always, it's necessary for me to thank The Lord God Almighty for using me as a vessel to share what I hope is a life changing and thought- provoking word for you. I must acknowledge my wonderful parents (Rita & Ray) who have both gone on to be with The Lord, as well as acknowledge my family and especially grandparents Mr. & Mrs. Joe Nathan Henderson and Mr. & Mrs. Sam Raby, Sr. My heart is eternally grateful to the Lord for blessing me with tremendous support, family and friends. And last, but certainly not the least, I must thank God for all of the wonderful mentors who continue to pour into my life and make me a better man. So to the Phenomenal Dr. Derrick E. Houston Sr., the anointed Rev. Roosevelt T. Hatcher Jr., the inspiring Elders Jackie & George W. Stewart and the dynamic Pastor Steve Green Sr.: I wish to thank you for your lasting impartations in my life.

Eternally grateful,

-Marc